The Difficult Horse

Understanding and solving riding, handling and behavioural problems

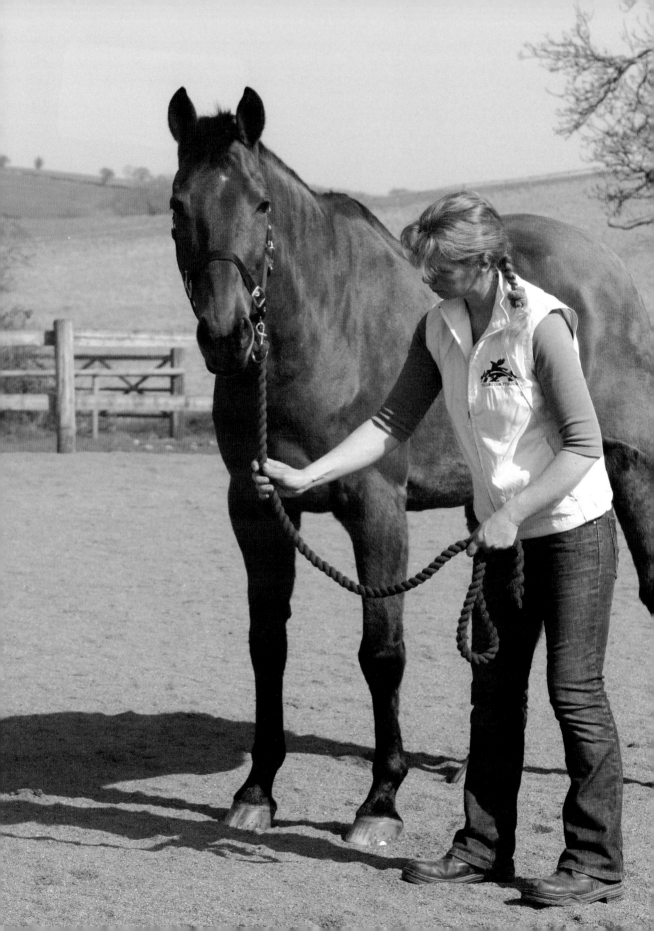

The Difficult Horse

Understanding and solving riding, handling and behavioural problems

Sarah Fisher & Karen Bush

THE CROWOOD PRESS

First published in 2012 by
The Crowood Press Ltd
Ramsbury, Marlborough
Wiltshire SN8 2HR

www.crowood.com

British Library Cataloguing-in-Publication Data
A catalogue record for this book is available from the British Library.

ISBN 978 1 84797 427 3

All photographs are © Sarah Fisher and Bob Atkins, except those on pages 11 and 23, which are by Bob Atkins, courtesy of *Horse & Rider* magazine.

Dedication
For the Horse, our greatest teacher and valued friend – Sarah
For Mum, with thanks for all the encouragement over the years – Karen

Acknowledgements
Our thanks go to Linda Tellington Jones, Robyn Hood, Peggy Cummings, Tina Constance, Mags Denness, Shelley Hawkins, Vicki McGarva, Tuesday Lewis, Rachel Denness, Amanda-Jayne Bell and Alison Bridge at *Horse & Rider* magazine for their help with this book – plus the horses Myrtle, Ginger, Equinox, Panj, Sage, Bailey, Wellington, Toto and Moomin.

Disclaimer
The authors and publisher do not accept any responsibility in any manner whatsoever for any error or omission, or any loss, damage, injury, adverse outcome or liability of any kind incurred as a result of the use of any of the information contained in this book, or reliance upon it.

Typeset by Jean Cussons Typesetting, Diss, Norfolk
Printed and bound in Singapore by Craft Print International

Contents

Foreword

I focus on working with the different personalities of each horse I ride, recognising that each one is an individual. I am continuously assessing where each horse's strengths and weaknesses lie, encouraging them into different outlines to develop correct muscle structure. The neck must be free and supple and the hind legs need to be active. I want the horse to be responsive to a light aid at all times, whether I am asking for an upward or downward transition.

The two basic principles are the same, regardless of the age of the horse or its level of experience – I want him to accept the leg and accept the rein, but I will vary the exercises according to the needs of each horse, as I want him to develop good physical balance and true self-carriage.

By sticking to those two principles, and ensuring that the hands are effective and elastic, the legs are effective and light, and that the aids are consistent, the horse is less confused. Both horse and rider can enjoy their time together, whether out hacking, schooling, jumping or competing in dressage, because the horse is happy and comfortable in his work. Even an Advanced horse may still be fearful of a competition environment, but he can become more confident in his rider and the environment if he understands that the partnership is strong via the correct use of the aids and good training has been established.

The Difficult Horse gives horse owners new ways of understanding the reasons for many unwanted behaviours, but perhaps more importantly it offers simple tools for change that anyone can learn. The aim of this book fits in with my own philosophy and beliefs; that a solid foundation and trust must be in place, that more complex tasks and movements should be developed slowly to ensure that softness and suppleness is maintained, that good balance is essential for physical and mental well being, and that battles can be avoided by going back a step at any stage in training if the horse is struggling with what he is being asked to do.

Lee Pearson CBE
Nine times Paralympic Dressage Gold Medallist
at Sydney 2000, Athens 2004, Beijing 2008

Introduction

Good horsemanship should look effortless, with horse and rider working in harmony to create a perfect partnership that is a pleasure to watch and a rewarding experience for both parties. This same principle should apply to all aspects of horse management.

Many problems occur because early warning signs that the horse was struggling were overlooked or ignored, or foundation steps in handling and training were rushed or not put in place at all. All horses benefit from a calm and quiet approach, but as unwanted behaviours begin to develop or become increasingly difficult to manage, our own fears and concerns can trigger more forceful handling. This in turn exacerbates the stress that the horse is already under, giving rise to more volatile reactions and the creation of new and more dangerous behaviours. It is this lack of understanding that causes the relationship between horse and man to break down, and compromises the horse's natural willingness to be a co-operative partner. As Xenophon stated so wisely in 400BC: 'Where knowledge ends, violence begins.'

There is always a reason for unwanted behaviour. The skill comes not in relying on force to push the horse through his difficulties, but in understanding the motive for that behaviour, and learning kind and effective techniques to help address his concerns. A horse that is able to think and to move freely through the body will be safer and easier to handle and ride than a horse that is stressed and/or physically compromised through ill-fitting equipment, inappropriate training and poor posture. Even if he lacks education, a horse that is calm is able to process and retain new information more easily than a horse that is tense, enabling you to work on advancing his skills rather than simply doing your best to work around or manage behavioural concerns on a daily basis.

Horses, like humans, have different personalities and different capabilities. Taking time to observe your horse and to learn how he uses his body language to communicate with you will help you to take any necessary steps to ensure that he is happy and comfortable in every aspect of his life.

Take time to observe your horse and understand his body language.

There is always a reason for unwanted behaviour; the owner needs to learn kind and effective techniques to address the horse's concerns.

When working through a problem remember that all behaviours are connected. For example, a horse that always carries himself in a high-headed frame may find it hard to stand still for the farrier, may move off at the mounting block the moment your foot is in the stirrup, and spook, spin or nap when ridden. He may also be difficult to handle from the ground. Teaching your horse to lower his head and release his top line, and learning exercises that you can do in the stable, in hand and under saddle that will strengthen his back, enabling him to work more efficiently and effectively, will go a long way to helping you address all the connected and unwanted behaviours. You may need to adapt the way you ride, manage and care for your horse, as there may be several contributory factors such as poor dentition, saddle fit and foot balance – but with increased knowledge you can help him reach his full potential whether you want a horse that is a pleasure to hack out in open countryside, or have more ambitious goals for yourself and your equine friend.

Key to Exercises

As well as suggesting specific exercises for particular problems, the reader is also referred to other exercises that might also be helpful. Below is an alphabetical list of the exercises given in this book, with the name of the problem opposite, where it is explained. We hope this will enable the reader to find these cross-referred exercises quickly and easily.

For example, in the problem 'Girthing issues' the exercise 'Belly Lifts' is given as helpful, and it is also suggested that the reader might try the exercise 'Lick of the Cow's Tongue': to find this exercise, locate it in the alphabetical list below, see which problem it is contained in, then locate that problem – most are in Part 3, the A–Z Directory. (The problems in the A–Z Directory are also listed alphabetically.)

Exercise	*Problem*
Balance Rein	Balance, on the forehand
Belly Lifts	Girthing issues
Body Wraps	In Chapter 5, section 'Equipment'
Caterpillar	Spooking
Clicker Targeting	In Chapter 5, section 'Targeting'
Clouded Leopard TTouch	In Chapter 5, section 'Body Work'
Crest Release	Outline
Deep Breathing	Over-excitable
Dingo	Leading, hanging back
Ear Work	Catching, difficulty in
Floating Forwards	Canter, disunited
Forelock Circles and Slides	Bridle, difficult to
Forelock Pulls	Outline
Homing Pigeon	Leading issues
Jellyfish Jiggles	Clipping
Jowl Release	In Chapter 4, section 'Read your Horse'
Labyrinth, The	Jumping, rushing fences
Leg Circles	Feet, difficult to shoe
Lick of the Cow's Tongue	Cold-backed
Llama TTouch	In Chapter 5, section 'Body Work'
Lying Leopard TTouch	In Chapter 5, section 'Body Work'
Meet and Melt	Outline
Mouth Work	Chewing

Narrow Spaces Exercise	Gateways, reluctant to go through
Neck Rocking	Outline
Neutral Pelvis	Canter, changing leads
Pick up Sticks	Stumbling
Promise Rope	Laziness
Promise Wrap	Standing still (halting while ridden)
Proprioception	In Chapter 3, section 'Lifestyle and Stress Management'
Raised Polework	Canter, favouring one lead
Reverse Reins	Bit evasions
Rotating the Pelvis	Rushing while ridden
Shoulder Presses	Jogging
Sliding Numnahs	Door, rushing through
Solo Polework	Clumsiness
Sternum Lifts	Balance, lack of physical
Stroking the Line	Nappiness
Stroking the Reins	Pulling while ridden
Tail Rolling	Stiffness
Tail Work	Standing still (halting in hand)
Tracing the Arc	Crookedness
Walking over Plastic	Water, fear of
Walking the S	Bucking
Walking under Wands	Travelling
Walking up Behind	Traffic shy
Wand Work	Grooming issues
Wither Rocking	Feet, difficult to pick up
Work over Different Surfaces	Bolting, while ridden
ZigZag	Jumping, running out

PART 1
IDENTIFYING PROBLEMS

1 Understanding the Equine Character

So what is a 'problem', and why do 'problems' arise? A 'problem' may be a minor irritation which inconveniences you, or something which prevents you from achieving certain goals – or it could be a serious behaviour that puts lives at risk.

From your horse's point of view, his actions may be a perfectly sensible response to a situation he finds himself in. The fact that they cause difficulties for you isn't his fault, and may not be yours either; but it is your responsibility as owner or carer to try to understand why he behaves as he does, and to help him learn how to cope with things he finds challenging in a way which is acceptable and safe for both of you. Failure to do so may lead to an escalation of his misbehaviour, and will certainly make it difficult for you to develop a true partnership.

Horses are not difficult on purpose: they do not intentionally set out to annoy us. On the contrary, the fact that they allow us to climb on their backs at all, let alone perform the physically and psychologically demanding tasks we ask of them, is a testament to their willingness and desire to co-operate as much as to their courage.

If you encounter any difficulties it is therefore important to consider all possible reasons for them; furthermore, as well as involving a certain amount of honest and objective self-assessment, it's also helpful to have a basic understanding of what makes your horse tick, both as an equine and as an individual.

UNDERSTANDING THE HORSE'S SURVIVAL TRAITS

Like dogs, the modern-day horse is a product of human intervention as well as of evolution, with intensive breeding for specific qualities giving rise to a whole range of different breeds. But horses have changed far less than our canine friends, partly because they have only been domesticated for around five to six thousand years as compared to around thirty thousand for dogs, and have not been subject to such constant and close human companionship.

It is also due to the fact that so many of the physical and behavioural traits which originally helped the horse survive – such as his sensitivity, being quick to react, co-operative, and able to gallop and jump – are also a key part of what makes him so good at the things we want to do with him. On the whole, horses cope remarkably well with the challenges of the modern-day environment, but domestication can sometimes be a thin veneer, and the very characteristics which make him so suited to our purposes can also underlie behaviours we consider undesirable.

Instinctive Responses

The horse's instinctive responses might be described as the five 'F's: flight, fight, freeze, faint and fool around. Regardless of where an animal is on the food chain, the majority of animals prefer to respond to fear by running away. It is not conducive to survival to engage in conflict, since the risk of injury and even death is increased through fighting. Only if the ability to flee is inhibited for any reason will the majority of animals, including people, either go into 'freeze' or respond with displays of aggression (fight).

When a horse is in 'freeze' his head will be raised, his nostrils may be flared and his eyes will be wide. You may also notice that his heart rate is elevated and his body is tense. Trying to push or beat a horse out of freeze can lead to an explosive reaction, risking injury to both horse and handler. It is far safer, as well as kinder, to encourage him to move a little by stroking along the lead line (or one rein if you are mounted) so as to gently turn his head, or to lower his head without forcing it down (*see* Exercise 'Stroking the Reins' – *see* Key to Exercises). He will probably jog or move off a little sharply for the first few strides and may go back into freeze after a couple of steps, but if you stay calm, and keep encouraging him to release through his body with your hands and/ or your own body, he will recover more quickly.

A horse that is defensive in his behaviour is not being 'dominant', but is under duress and communicating high levels of concern. If pushed, he may 'faint'. This fear response can be triggered by forceful handling – when loading, for example – and some people sadly believe that the horse is lying down because he 'knows' that by dropping to the floor he cannot be forced into the lorry. 'Faint' is an indicator of extreme levels of stress, and no horse should ever be pushed to this point.

'Fool around' is often misinterpreted as the horse being 'naughty' or lacking focus. The horse may grab the lead line, toss his head around, paw the ground, fidget and so on. It is usually triggered by confusion because the horse is struggling with the situation, but it can be due to anticipation of something either pleasurable or worrying, and is often accompanied by areas of tension through the body. Even if, for example, your horse is working well initially or is enjoying being groomed, if he starts to fool around, stop what you are doing. You may have worked him for too long – even though you may have considered the session brief – or have touched a sensitive area, or he may have become distracted because he did not understand what was being asked of him. Look for the pattern: there will be one, and by noting when and why your horse starts to lose focus or change his behaviour, you can make any necessary alterations to the way you handle and train him.

Physical Senses

Modern-day horses may not look much like their distant ancestors, but their senses – vision, hearing, taste and smell, and touch – remain much the same, and are designed to aid in survival. The way a horse perceives the world around him can differ slightly from the way in which we do, and may affect his response to the environments and situations he finds himself in.

Vision

Eyesight is one of the horse's most important senses with regard to warning of potential danger. The positioning of the eyes to the side of the head provides good all-round vision – about 350 degrees, with 'blind spots' created by the head and body just in front, at the back of the head, and immediately to the rear – hence the advice always to approach from the side, so as to avoid startling him.

If something seen with one eye catches the horse's attention, by turning his head to look at it he can use binocular vision (both eyes at the same time), which improves his depth perception. But once the object is within three or four feet, the length of his nose begins to obscure it, and to continue looking at it he needs to turn his head again and observe with one eye. Visual information can be transferred from one eye to the other: nevertheless, it is often noticed that a horse will spook at an object he has already seen when passing it for the first time in the opposite direction and seeing it with the other eye.

Horses are very sensitive to movement – not just of people, animals and inanimate objects, but also of shadows moving on the ground or light reflected from the surface of water. The ability to detect motion is greater in their peripheral vision, and this, combined with a reduced ability to see in detail in this area and the wide field of vision, can explain why horses may sometimes appear to spook at nothing.

Although better than us at seeing in low light conditions, horses' eyes adjust less quickly to abrupt changes, which is why they may be reluctant to enter a dark stable or trailer, or may refuse at a show jump or cross-country fence positioned in a shady area.

Some individuals may be long- or short-sighted, and as with humans, ageing can lead to a deterioration in eyesight. The gradual loss of sight in one eye is generally coped with well – often so well that the owner doesn't realize a problem exists. Given time and good care, some horses even learn to manage well with a loss of sight in both eyes. However, horses with poor vision may be more noise-sensitive, and anyway care must also be taken to warn them of your approach through the use of your voice.

When riding, the horse's head carriage can also affect vision; when asked to work in an outline it can limit what he is able to see ahead, in the same way as your own vision is inhibited if you look downwards. If he is overbent, it decreases still more. For a horse, working in an outline requires not just correct training of his physique, but that he places great trust in the rider to keep him safe, both from possible predators and from bumping into anything.

Hearing

Our own hearing range is around 20Hz–20kHz, and that of a horse is around 55Hz–33kHz: this means that he can hear some high-pitched sounds that we can't, but not some of the lower frequency ones. For example, depending on how close and loud it is, he may be able to hear, and be disturbed by, ultrasonic rodent repellers if you use this form of pest control.

Each ear can be rotated to give all-round hearing without having to move the head, and its funnel shape helps in focusing on a particular sound, just as you might cup a hand round your own ear to shut out extraneous noise to help you hear what someone is saying.

Music is often played on yards, and studies have shown that it can be beneficial in reducing stress in elephants in zoos, soothing dogs in rescue shelters, and calming newly weaned foals. But avoid leaving radios on constantly, and choose the sort of music which horses show definite preferences for – rhythmic and calming instrumental melodies. Consider volume as well: sounds can be muffled to a certain extent by pinning the ears back, but can't be shut out altogether.

Some individuals appear more reactive to sound than others, but sudden noises can startle any horse – not just extra loud ones such as fireworks, shotguns and bird scarers, but dropped mucking-out tools and slammed doors too, which can contribute to raising a horse's stress levels. Noises which he finds worrying or irritating, but which he can't identify, may also cause increasing anxiety. Adrenalin can increase noise sensitivity, and a horse that is stressed will be more reactive to sound.

Equine sensitivity to sound can be usefully employed: for example, a low-pitched, soothing tone with long drawn-out syllables can have a calming, steadying effect – although bear in mind that shouting and high-pitched tones can have the opposite result. Talking while working around your horse will ensure that he knows where you are at all times if you move into a 'blind spot' or if he has vision issues, and when approaching him this can also be a more reliable form of identification for him than your appearance or smell, both of which can change from day to day (and even during it) depending on what deodorants, scents, aftershaves and soaps you use and what clothes you take off or put on.

As with vision, hearing can deteriorate with age, or be compromised by health issues. Never trim the hairs inside the ears, as they have a sensory function and help keep out dirt and flies. Note whether an ear is flicked towards the source of a sound: reduced or loss of hearing will affect his ability to respond to verbal cues, and may cause him to be more easily startled by anything approaching from the rear.

Taste and Smell

Taste and smell are very closely linked: they are well developed senses which, together with mobile lips, enable horses to differentiate between different foodstuffs, and to reject those which are unpalatable. Smells can be detected over far greater distances than humans are capable of, and with considerably greater acuity; scent recognition plays an important role in greeting and identifying other horses – for example between mares and foals – and in detecting possible threats. Strange, strong or unusual smells can cause alarm, where the horse is reluctant to approach the source of the smell, while a change of feedstuff or drinking water, or the addition of supplements or medications, may lead to the horse refusing to eat or drink.

Can horses smell fear? Although nervousness is also betrayed by body language, it is quite possible that chemicals produced and emanated by the body in response to stress can be detected. As with hearing, stressed horses are likely to have an increased sense of smell.

Touch

Horses are highly sensitive to touch, able to detect as tiny and light a thing as a fly landing on them, and to twitch the skin to dislodge it; some areas of the body are more sensitive than others – the flanks, beneath the belly and between the thighs, for example.

They enjoy having certain areas scratched with the fingertips, and field companions can often be observed enjoying mutual grooming sessions. When using touch as a form of praise and reward, stroking and scratching is preferred to patting, which can seem abrupt and may be perceived as a punishing action.

The long whiskers on the head also function as sensory organs: deeply embedded in the skin, each is rooted in a specialized follicle with a rich supply of nerves. These help foals locate the teat when suckling, they aid grazing by determining the length of grass and proximity of the ground, and help prevent facial damage by warning of nearby objects; it has even been suggested that they may be able to detect sound and vibrations. Although little research has been done with regard to horses, these whiskers – or 'vibrissae' – have been shown to be sufficiently important as a sensory organ in other animals that trimming them has been banned in Germany.

2 Investigating Problems

Behavioural problems in horses can have various underlying causes; these might include the effects of stress, the influence of genetics (inherited behavioural traits), physical problems, or previous experiences.

THE UNDERLYING CAUSES OF UNDESIRABLE BEHAVIOURS

Stress

Stress, both physical and psychological, can be a major cause of undesirable behaviours. The relatively short amount of time the horse has been domesticated has done little to equip him for the modern world and the increasingly artificial environments in which he is kept today.

Individual horses react differently to stressful situations, with some coping better than others, depending on factors such as temperament and previous experience. Where stress is ongoing as opposed to an isolated event, the constant release of the stress hormones which prepare the body for action can have an adverse effect on health. As well as increasing the risk of colic, gastric ulcers, laminitis and diarrhoea, they can inhibit the immune system and growth, reduce reproductive capacity, affect bone integrity and hoof growth, and may lead to the appearance of stereotypies such as crib biting and weaving, and behaviours such as spookiness. Common stressors and stress management are discussed in more detail in Part 2.

Inherited Behavioural Traits

Just as physical characteristics can be inherited, so can behavioural traits. They can be breed related, and/or passed on through family bloodlines – though it is important not to tar all horses with the same brush. It is easy to develop subconscious prejudices based on previous experiences and popular mythology, and these can often be unfounded. Yes, temperamental chestnuts, flighty Arabs and lazy, unflappable cobs do exist – but there are just as many placid chestnuts, laid-back Arabs and reactive cobs, so it's important to view each and every horse as an individual.

Bear in mind also that environment, handling and training each play a critical role in how a horse behaves, and where less desirable traits such as fearfulness, reactivity or a predisposition to various stereotypies have been inherited, they become even more important in helping the horse to develop into a balanced personality.

Physical Problems

An out-of-character behaviour can often be due to physical discomfort, especially if it appears suddenly; where low-grade pain is concerned, behaviours can be slower to develop and a link between the two may be less obvious. Horses also have varying pain thresholds, so what can be borne by one may be intolerable for another.

As a first step in tackling undesirable behaviours, always ask a vet to check for any physical problems so that health issues can be remedied or eliminated as a cause. Even if nothing is found, don't rule it out completely but continue to monitor and observe closely, as getting to the root of health issues is not always straightforward; some ailments can be difficult to diagnose, and you may have nothing more than intuition to guide you. Be prepared to ask for referrals and further tests if necessary – this can be a time when you will be grateful that your horse is insured.

Although an improvement may be noticed, removal of the source of the discomfort does not always lead to the immediate resolution of a problem, as the horse may still anticipate, or make associations with pain which can take time to change.

Horses were never designed to be ridden; the spine and associated musculature is intended to help suspend the large and bulky belly, not to support the weight of a rider or to sustain the exaggerated athletic

Early experiences both good and bad will influence how the horse matures – forceful handling of a youngster can trigger defensive responses. Long schooling sticks are ideal for initiating contact with any horses that are threatened by the presence of humans as they enable you to keep a distance and allow the horse to move away if necessary.

efforts and way of moving that we demand. The spine is not the only part of the body that can feel the strain, so as well as constant observation and awareness of changes in movement, willingness, temperament, posture and general appearance that may indicate physical health issues, a case could be made for preventive health care, with physiotherapy and other modalities being usefully employed for the maintenance of physical wellbeing, and not just when a problem is suspected.

Previous Experiences

Horses have good memories, and can form deep and lasting associations, particularly for traumatic events. Even when the cause of an unpleasant experience has been removed, the horse may continue to anticipate it for a long time to come – for example, continuing to spook at a certain point on a ride where a bag flapped across the road and scared him, or to flinch, pull faces or nip when being saddled if it has previously been a source of pain.

Likewise, lack of experience can predispose to difficulties too: horses that have been kept in relatively isolated circumstances, or were orphaned or weaned early, are more likely to be fearful and to exhibit unwanted behaviours. Over-handling orphaned youngsters, particularly if they have grown up without the company of another youngster in their early

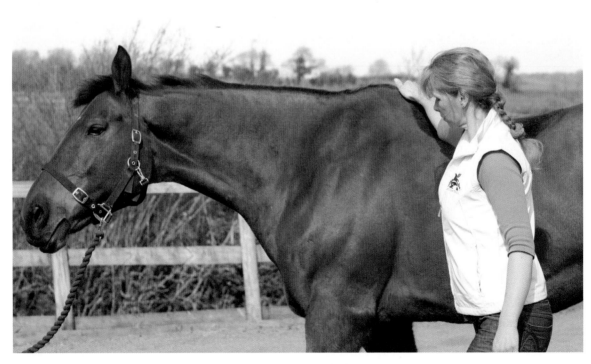

If early signs of concern are ignored when the horse is touched on specific parts of the body he has no choice but to increase his body language. Punishing the horse for his reactions reinforces his anxieties, breaks down the relationship and is likely to trigger more volatile outbursts.

years, can give rise to extremely dangerous behaviours as they mature.

Although they may be more settled and established in their behaviour, older as well as young horses can be adversely affected by negative experiences – though remember that it is also possible to provide positive experiences, producing changes in behaviour for the better.

RESOLVING PROBLEMS

Do all problems need resolving? Equally, is it possible to resolve all problems? And should you give up on a problem, or persevere at all costs? The answer to each of these questions is both yes and no, and depends on a number of factors.

Warning Signs

Some behaviours may not directly affect you, or may be sufficiently minor that it is easy to overlook and live with them. But any atypical behaviour can be an indicator that all is not well in your horse's world, so every effort should be made to discover and remedy the cause. Failure to do so will affect your horse's quality of life, may affect his health and performance, and could lead to more serious developments – many major behavioural problems can trace their origins back to seemingly small and trivial beginnings.

Achieving Success

Can all problems be cured? It may be possible to resolve some problems so successfully that they don't occur again, but this isn't always the case, and you should be realistic about how much change you can achieve. It may only be possible to partially remedy some undesirable behaviours, and others may prove impossible, depending on a variety of factors; these might include:

- The nature of the problem
- How long it has been in existence – the more ingrained a behaviour is, the longer it may take to remedy it, and the more difficult this may be
- Your expertise and skill
- How feasible it is to make changes to the environment and management
- The presence of any ongoing physical trauma or health issues

Stereotypies such as box walking, weaving, cribbing and windsucking can often prove particularly troublesome to eliminate, and may sometimes continue even when the underlying cause has been dealt with. These behaviours trigger the release of 'feel-good' chemicals in the brain, and it is thought that consequently there can be an element of addiction involved. But as any smoker trying to quit the habit will tell you, it is not just about chemicals – established habit can play a part, too.

Sometimes horses will revert to behaviours you thought had been 'cured' when placed under pressure or stressed, so it may be necessary not just to change the environment and daily care, but to rethink the work the horse is asked to do.

Working Through a Problem

Sometimes you may need to decide whether it would be best to give up on a problem, rather than persevering at all costs. While working through and resolving difficulties can be an immensely rewarding process, which can lead to the forging of close bonds between you and your horse, in some instances it may not always be feasible or safe for you to do so.

Much depends on the nature of the problem, whether you are skilled enough to deal with it, or are able to find expert help, and have the time available both to work on the problem and to wait until it has sufficiently improved to a level where you are satisfied. Finances can also be an aspect: some problems may be expensive to resolve.

If a behaviour has eroded your nerve, even after it has to all intents and purposes been resolved, you may continue to experience feelings of anxiety. Although modalities such as TellingtonTouch (TTEAM) and Neuro Linguistic Programming (NLP) can be brilliant in helping to develop confidence and restore damaged trust, sometimes a change of owner is the best solution for everyone. Persisting when intuition and common sense tell you it isn't something you feel comfortable doing may lead to another hiatus, and one which may have more serious consequences. However, do not pass on a problem without telling a potential buyer about it – and for your horse's sake be very careful about any choice of new home.

Professional Assistance

At what point should you consider getting professional help? Never battle on alone if you are struggling to cope, or failing to make any headway in resolving a problem, or if it is becoming worse. There is nothing wrong about admitting that you don't feel knowledgeable or able enough, or are too nervous to deal with a problem by yourself. Seeking out expert and competent help is the sensible course of action!

Sometimes you may find that several people come forward willing to offer advice – but be careful about which to accept: even 'experienced' people aren't necessarily knowledgeable, and those who subscribe to dangerous, inhumane or outmoded practices are definitely to be avoided. This isn't always as easy as it sounds, especially when the person offering the advice has perceived status and acceptance, and you may need to resist well meaning but not always well informed pressure from friends and acquaintances, for your own and your horse's wellbeing.

Flexibility, adaptability, open-mindedness and a willingness to try different approaches are important, but any advice or training method you follow must suit both you and your horse: it must be humane, and must absolutely avoid any bullying, coercive techniques.

Just as important as training methods, you need to trust and feel comfortable with the trainer, too: no matter how good they may be, if there is any kind of personality conflict you will not get the best result. Sometimes people have an aversion to a certain breed, type, colour or sex of horse, and this can lead to a certain rigidity of thinking and consequently poor handling or inappropriate training techniques. Empathy with you and your horse is vital, and a trainer needs to be able to communicate well with both of you, and to show you how to replicate the work he or she does, rather than keep it a jealously guarded secret.

Finding the right advice may take time: if necessary give your horse a holiday while you search for it. Whether you find someone through personal recommendation, advertisement, Yellow Pages or online, don't engage their services until you have first discussed your problem, asked how they intend to work through it, investigated the likely outcome, found out how much all this is going to cost you, and in particular have watched them at work with other horses and riders, because what people say is not always what they do.

Obviously it is more convenient for everyone – and will be cheaper, too – if you can find someone reasonably local; but if you can't find

Enlist the help of someone who can help you with your horse, but make sure that it is someone who will hear you and work with you, rather than trying to ram their own opinions down your throat. You should feel supported and inspired by any person who helps you, and not be made to feel intimidated or fearful in any way.

the right person on your doorstep, be prepared either to travel to them, or to pay for them to come to you.

Don't Blame Yourself!

No one becomes an expert overnight: on your journey to becoming a knowledgeable and experienced horseperson, it is inevitable that you will make some errors – although it is to be hoped that you won't make too many, or of too serious a nature. Sometimes problems are not of your making, but inherited from previous owners.

If your horse does develop a problematic behaviour it is important not to go on a guilt trip about it: rather, award yourself a pat on the back for noticing it, and deciding to do something positive about it. Feeling excessively guilty or sorry for the horse can inhibit the growth of a balanced relationship between you, and is likely to interfere with your ability to make the right decisions and take the correct actions.

PART 2
PROBLEM SOLVING

3 Understanding Horse Behaviour

Labels are given to equine behaviour as a way of identifying various issues, but this can limit our ability to help the horse, as they can cause us to overlook the reasons why the behaviour became established in the first place.

Two labels commonly used (and frequently incorrectly applied) by many trainers and owners with regard to behaviour are 'submissive' or 'dominant'. These labels can be misleading, and certainly when it comes to 'dominant' behaviour, can trigger inappropriate handling and unsuccessful behaviour modification techniques which not only break down the equine/human bond, but fail to address the underlying reasons that caused the more dominant behaviour to manifest itself in the first place.

In terms of behaviour, the true application of the word 'dominant' should be to describe a very specific behaviour around a resource – such as food for example – when another being or beings are present. 'Dominant' should never be used to describe a personality, and even if the word is being correctly used in the right context, our own perception of that behaviour may be incorrect. For example, a horse which expresses what we may view as aggressive behaviour around food may in fact be sore in the mouth, suffer from gut problems, or be stiff and therefore less mobile when grazing or eating hay in the field. If the horse has been stabled for long periods of time and subjected to poor management and an inappropriate feeding schedule, he may have learnt to become more protective and reactive around

his feed, which has become the highlight of his day. If he experiences any stress or discomfort when being groomed, tacked up or ridden, his hostile response to you approaching him in the field or stable may in fact be linked to a negative association with you, rather than an aggressive action intended to keep you away from his food.

Once applied, labels also tend to focus attention on that particular issue, with other, less obvious ones, which may overlap, going unnoticed or ignored, while positive and appropriate behaviours may be overlooked and go unrewarded, which seriously limits the possibility for change. Another drawback with labels is that they tend to stick and can be difficult to remove, influencing all future work with the horse.

THE BEHAVIOUR SPECTRUM

In order for us to develop appropriate and successful strategies to help horses, it can be more beneficial to look at behaviour in a different way.

First, to take the earlier example, how about replacing the words 'dominant' and 'submissive' with 'extrovert' and 'introvert' instead? This immediately changes the way in which you view the behaviour, and a rather black and white image is replaced with one which is open to a wider variety of interpretations and doesn't conjure up images of violence and subjugation which will invariably colour your response. Bear

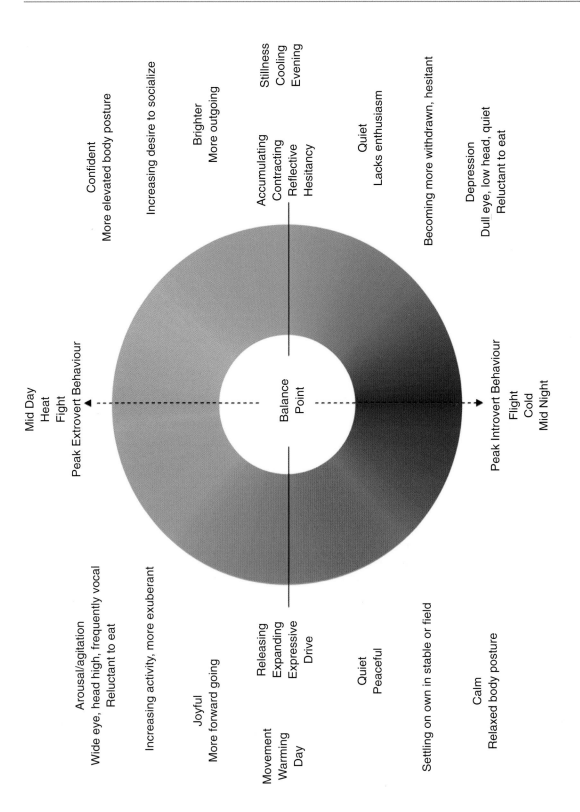

The behaviour spectrum.

in mind we are talking about behaviour at this point, not trying to establish whether a horse is introvert or extrovert in his nature.

Secondly, few horses remain in one state all of the time. Behaviour is not fixed, but in a state of constant change from minute to minute, and day to day. Understanding that behaviour is a continuum and not fixed can open our eyes to seeing horses in a new way, and help us understand how we can use the many tools at our disposal to bring each horse into a better state of emotional and mental balance. If we think of extreme introvert behaviour as being at one end of a spectrum, with extreme extrovert behaviour at the other, we can see that most horses (and people) are generally continuously moving through that spectrum to some degree, depending on many factors including the current environment, interaction with other horses and people, diet, training techniques and so on.

For further clarity, let's apply colour to that spectrum: at one point on the scale the colour is dark blue (excessively introvert), and at another it is orange (excessively extrovert). If you consider this spectrum as a circle rather than as a straight line it will also serve as a reminder that the horse can move from one extreme state to another in either direction, or even directly across the diameter of the circle, without necessarily moving through the entire colour range first. When moving around the circle you'll notice that the colours merge into each other with no obvious definitions between each shade, just as there are often no clear boundaries or beginnings and endings between behaviours.

The balance point can be placed at the centre of a horizontal line drawn across the circle. A horse which is well balanced in temperament will be in, or close to, that middle point, although he will still continue to move through the spectrum according to the influence of a variety of factors. These factors will also dictate to a degree both how far and how quickly he

moves, and whether he is able to return to a more balanced state or not.

A horse that we would generally consider to be in balance would be able to move effortlessly through these phases without the need for much intervention from his owner or carer. For example, there will be times when a horse is exuberant and joyful, such as when he is first turned out, but also times when he may be hesitant, such as going into a horsebox or when approached by a vet. He may be active when ridden (extrovert), but peaceful and calm in his stable (introvert).

Most horses, like people, will of course have a tendency to be naturally more introvert or extrovert in character and therefore behaviour, but problems tend to arise when the horse is stuck in one phase and has moved, or is moving, further away from the point of balance in the spectrum. If this occurs or has occurred in the past we may see more obvious signs of imbalance.

These examples of extrovert and introvert attributes are by no means comprehensive, and are not necessarily exclusive to either behaviour or phase. They are intended merely as a guide to help you adopt an observant and flexible approach, and to enable you to start thinking about what sort of work and training techniques may be most useful to bring your horse into a better balance.

Always remember that behaviours overlap and merge, and that any experience the horse has can drive him in one direction or the other, regardless of the starting point within the spectrum. For example, quiet horses are often 'pushed' too quickly, and one which is naturally more introvert may be forced to become more outwardly reactive in order to make his fear or confusion known. Similarly, a naturally outgoing and tactile horse subjected to forceful handling and aversive training techniques in a bid to curb his exuberant behaviour may shut down and become withdrawn as a result.

Looking at behaviour in this way will help you

Extreme Extrovert	Extreme Introvert
Heat – sweating	Cold – cold extremities
Constant movement	Reluctance to move
Plunging, striking, stamping, rearing, spinning	In freeze
Hard mouthing/biting/kicking	Pulling faces and retreating
Excessive vocalization	Silence
Needing constant engagement, activity, food	Consistently withdrawn, picky eater
Body posture consistently erect	Body posture consistently low
Red eyes	White of eyes showing
On constant alert	Shut down
Moving forwards, striking, standing ground when unsure	Drawing back when unsure
Manic behaviour	Depression
Tendency to fight	Tendency to flight

to understand that the horse is not necessarily making deliberate choices about how he responds to the environment that humans have created for him. We would encourage you all to start making notes about how the horses that you work with and/or own respond to a variety of situations. As already explained, ideally you should see a mix of both introvert and extrovert behaviours, depending on circumstance and even the time of the day. Begin trying to develop or think of strategies that can help you have a positive influence on the behaviour that you see at the time.

LIFESTYLE AND STRESS MANAGEMENT

Most horses live a very artificial lifestyle which is not ideally suited to them. Consequently, many suffer from some degree of stress, although the owner/carer may be unaware of this. Stress can affect any horse, whether young or old, ridden or retired, competing or ridden for pleasure. Some horses learn to cope with, or adapt to, the various stressors in their lives better than others, but the effects of even low grade levels of stress can be cumulative, and the carer is often surprised when an animal which has seemed calm and contented suddenly exhibits undesirable behaviours.

Removing stressors and creating as natural a lifestyle as possible are factors that play a key part in resolving difficulties, as well as minimizing the potential for them to arise. The following are the most common ones, and will influence where your horse moves on the behaviour spectrum (*see* previous section) and can be the cause of, or contribute to, unwanted behaviours arising. Often more than one of these may need to be addressed.

Over-confinement

Horses have evolved to spend most of their time

moving around browsing for food, so keeping them turned out for as much of the time as possible is one of the most important aspects of their management, both physiologically and mentally, and will prevent the occurrence of many problems. In winter it can be tempting to overcoddle your horse and keep him stabled, but he won't appreciate being confined to quarters. Rug technology is excellent these days, so even if he is clipped you should be able to find something that will keep him warm and allow him to be out in all weathers for a large part of each day.

Although it may not be suitable or feasible for everyone, the turnout area can be given added interest if a 'Paradise Paddock' system can be set up. As well as helping to increase the amount of self-exercise your horse takes – important for biological processes such as circulation of blood and lymph – it can add an element of discovery, encouraging a more thorough exploration of the environment.

If it does become necessary to stable your horse for an extended period, create a stimulating environment for him by providing a safety mirror and horse toys, food and treat dispensers, whole swedes and slow-release forage feeders, to keep him occupied.

There is evidence to suggest that some horses kept stabled for much or even all of the time during winter may suffer from seasonal affective disorder (SAD), especially if worked in a covered school as well, which further reduces the amount of natural light they are exposed to. Daylight elicits the release of serotonin, a neurotransmitter that plays a part in regulating sleep, mood and appetite: animals affected by SAD may show signs of irritability, poor concentration levels, anxiety and depression, and be slower to learn new things. Not all

A calm and happy horse will be content to graze in the field and will not be 'clingy' with other horses or pester or bully his companions.

horses are affected, although it is thought that emotional or physical traumas may trigger the condition.

If you suspect that behaviours may be linked to SAD, remember that they will be seasonal rather than all year round. Keeping your horse turned out is the obvious solution to the problem, but if he has to be kept stabled for some reason, using a special light box offers an alternative.

Companionship

Horses are gregarious by nature, and long periods of isolation with no social stimulation and interaction will be stressful as well as boring for them. They may feel insecure, and will be more likely to develop stereotypies such as weaving and box- or fence-walking, and may call out to others or attempt to join them by breaking through or jumping over any barriers in their way.

Overcrowding can be just as stressful as lack of company, and may lead to territorial aggression being shown towards others. From the point of view of providing adequate space as much as maintaining grazing, consider a minimum stocking rate of 2–2.5 acres per horse.

Changes in company will also upset group dynamics, and care should be taken when introducing newcomers; groups that are constantly changing can cause some horses to be in a state of constant stress.

When stabled, partitions between each box will allow horses to see and interact with their neighbours – although sometimes there can be conflicts between individuals, which can be stressful for both, in which case move one to a different stable with company he finds more congenial. Where partitions aren't feasible, fitting a safety mirror appears to be an acceptable alternative for many horses: positioned at head height about half a metre

(two feet or so) from the door is a preferred location – though it shouldn't be close to where food is placed, to avoid any perceived competition.

Inappropriate Diet

The equine digestive system is adapted to deal with large quantities of low-grade nutrients ingested over long periods of time, and left to their own devices horses will spend up to sixteen hours out of twenty-four in grazing activities. If sufficient forage isn't available, it can lead to health issues such as colic and gastric ulcers, as well as feelings of hunger, boredom and frustration. Some horses may adopt behaviours such as cribbing, wood chewing and windsucking, or may eat their bedding or their own droppings.

Fibre in the diet also plays an important part in the synthesis of B vitamins, which are essential to a number of bodily processes including supporting brain and nervous system function. If it is necessary to limit food intake for reasons of weight control, try soaking hay for twelve hours as this will leach out most of the nutrients – including calories – allowing your horse to continue to receive an adequate forage ration.

Feeding energy-rich products that are in excess of your horse's requirements can also result in difficult behaviour and physical problems. Many owners overestimate workload; and remember that manufacturers' feeding suggestions are only guidelines, and should be adjusted as appropriate for the individual animal. If you need help devising a suitable diet for your horse, or have a query about a product, most manufacturers have free telephone helplines where you can speak to an equine nutritionist and ask for advice.

It's not just what you feed, but how you feed which can contribute to your horse's wellbeing. Feeding from the ground is preferable to using haynets and mangers, as it will ensure correct jaw alignment and more even tooth wear; it allows the sinuses to drain down, and won't lead to incorrect musculature forming on the underside of the neck. With horses that eat their forage ration quickly, ground-level feeding systems are available which slow them down, duplicating the grazing process.

Workload

Conformation may limit what a horse is comfortably and confidently able to do: he also needs to be temperamentally as well as physically suited to the work he is expected to perform. While a degree of ambition in the rider can be a good thing, if the horse is constantly under pressure to work at a level beyond his abilities, his confidence and willingness will be affected.

Just because you are not tired, it doesn't mean your horse isn't feeling fatigued. Overworking often happens, frequently without the rider realizing it; and especially if muscle groups are stiff and unaccustomed to the usage it can cause considerable discomfort and soreness. It is neither necessary nor desirable to ask your horse to work at maximum ability all the time: this can be mentally as well as physically demanding, and create negative associations both with you and the place where he is worked.

When teaching anything new, keep the work sessions short, rather than overloading him mentally and physically with lots of new information. Developing all the skills necessary to perform an action may also take many lessons, rather than a single one, to establish. It's always better to stop a little sooner than risk overdoing things – and as the brain continues to process information for up to twenty-four hours, you may find that when you return to an exercise that your horse previously struggled with, there is a definite improvement.

Unbalanced incisors can cause a horse to stiffen on one rein and become resistant under saddle.

Teeth

Do you know the saying 'Never look a gift horse in the mouth'? Well, ignore it! The mouth should be your first port of call if you are working with, or being offered, a horse with behavioural concerns, since many problem behaviours can be linked to issues in the mouth.

The time when a young horse is changing his teeth is often when he is asked to accept a bit and begin his education under saddle. A retained cap can cause a major problem for youngsters, and even if they are not being started under saddle, can trigger leading problems, as pressure from the noseband of a headcollar can cause discomfort.

Sharp edges, high or broken teeth, and wolf teeth are just some of the problems we have found in horses that display unwanted behaviours such as rearing, bolting, napping and bucking. As well as having a direct impact on general attitude, the balance of the mouth will influence how the horse develops muscle and the way he moves under saddle. For example, the lower jaw moves slightly forwards when the horse lowers his neck; uneven teeth, coupled with a tight noseband, can inhibit this natural movement and the horse will have no choice but to work above the bit as a result. If the noseband is loose he will have to open his mouth to allow the jaw to move, and may then be labelled as a horse that is trying to evade the bit.

The correlation between the mouth and movement is often overlooked, but a skilled equine dental technician can tell what is going on in the mouth by simply observing the posture and movement of the horse. They will hopefully spend some considerable time addressing the problems, so a flying visit from someone who works with several horses in a short space of time is probably best avoided.

High teeth at the back of the jaw often go undetected, and even some people who are qualified to work on the horse's teeth overlook the importance of the balance of the incisors because they may be limited in their own education. This applies to some vets as well as those trained in equine dentistry, so if you feel something is amiss, it may be worth getting a second opinion from someone with a greater skill level. Watch how your horse eats: you should note that he moves his jaw in a circular motion *in both directions* over the course of a day. If he only ever moves the jaw in one direction it is likely that he has some dental problems. You can also gently palpate your horse's jowls in line with the teeth as this will provoke a reaction in a horse that has sharp edges. You can also check for sensitivity around the hinge point of the jaw, as this can also be an indicator of an unbalanced mouth.

Some horses drop their feed if they eat too quickly so this is not necessarily the sign of a problem in the mouth, but if your horse drops wads of part-chewed food and has other problems too – such as sensitivity to contact around the head, issues with bridling, a dull eye, resistance on one rein, working consistently above the bit and so on – it is likely that he has a dental problem.

Ill-Fitting Saddlery

Most riders appreciate the importance of a correctly fitting saddle, yet it is another area often overlooked as a source of difficult behaviour. Depending on the materials used, the panels of the saddle may become compressed with use: and horses will change in shape throughout the year, putting on or losing weight according to the season, and increasing or losing muscle depending on the amount and type of work being done. Consequently, the saddle that fitted perfectly

Horses with thick lips will be more comfortable in a narrow bit.

when first bought may not sit so well a few months down the line, so regular checks should be made.

The position of the stirrup bars can also cause problems for the horse and some saddles may be far too narrow through the gullet, so it isn't a simple case of merely establishing if the front arch clears the withers or whether the points of the tree impair movement when checking the fit of your saddle. There are many points to consider, including the balance of the saddle and whether or not it is the right size for you as well as your horse.

Bitting is often another troublesome area: a large mouthpiece, for example, is not, as is often assumed, necessarily a kind one if the horse has a short mouth or large tongue. Saddlery also needs to be correctly adjusted if it is to do its job without causing discomfort. We see many horses with ill-fitting bridles, and browband fit is as important as that of the saddle and bit; if too tight it will cause pressure on the poll and around the back of the ears.

This is a large as well as an important subject, and all owners/carers/riders should make the effort to expand their knowledge of it through consulting books, as well as seeking expert advice from a good saddler and/or bit manufacturer.

Physical Discomfort

With any behaviour, it is essential to eliminate pain as a cause or contributory factor. Physical discomfort can be caused by all sorts of things – sharp teeth, saddlery that doesn't fit, injuries, an unbalanced or rough rider, bad shoeing, soreness from not being fit enough or sufficiently well prepared to cope with an activity, injury or illness ... the list of possible causes is endless. Like us, horses differ in their pain threshold: some can't cope with much at

all, while others are incredibly stoic and will put up with a considerable amount for a long period of time before it all becomes too much. Depending on the degree and cause of the pain, as well as the individual, the response may vary from depression and perceived laziness to more extreme and dangerous behaviours such as biting, bucking and kicking.

Never assume that a physical problem doesn't exist until it has been reliably proved that it doesn't. Some low grade physical problems can be very difficult to put a finger on; making a diagnosis can also be tricky if they are intermittent in nature, and it may be necessary to seek specialist veterinary advice to get to the bottom of an issue.

Age-Related Physical Changes

Physical changes such as joint stiffness, a dropped back and deterioration of vision and hearing will invariably occur as your horse grows older, but as they are often gradual in onset they may not be noticed until some kind of difficulty is encountered. Just because your senior horse is 'doing well for his age' it doesn't mean he is enjoying himself – the fact that he is still rising to the challenges you present him with may be a reflection of his personality rather than his physical capacity for the work. Be ready to tone down the more physically demanding aspects before he has to let you know in no uncertain terms that he is struggling to cope.

Remember, too, that young horses will also be affected by physical and psychological changes as they grow, and anything you do with them should take these into account. Although five years is generally accepted as being the age at which horses attain adult development, some may mature much later than this, and until full maturity is reached the

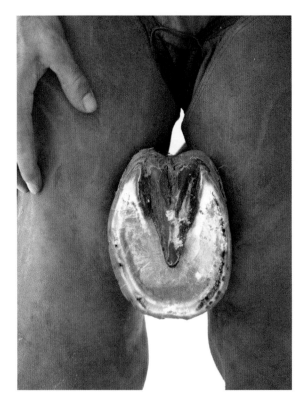

Correct foot balance is crucial for mental and physical wellbeing. Note how the frog had developed before the foot was balanced. The shape of the frog can give you a lot of information about how the horse is loading his hoof.

emphasis should be on educating rather than working them.

Poor Riding

The rider can also be a source of problem behaviour in the horse. A good position is absolutely crucial, enabling you to assist the horse rather than impede or interfere with him, and to communicate clearly and receive feedback from him. The pursuit of perfecting your posture should be an ongoing one; a concept which you actively pursue rather than just pay lip-service to. You will need assistance with this, as it is easy for your body to deceive you into thinking you are sitting correctly when in fact you aren't. Trying the proprioception exercise on page 36 demonstrates this very well, and will help you understand why it is difficult to work on positional corrections

by yourself, as well as how easy it is for bad habits to creep in unnoticed. An incorrect posture can feel 'right', which makes it much harder to change, because when you do, the correct posture will feel odd, possibly a little uncomfortable, and generally 'wrong'. This is also a lesson to remember when trying to change postural habits and behaviours in your horse!

Regular lessons from a knowledgeable instructor are ideal: if you can't afford them as often as you would like, ask a friend to watch and help you with some of the basics such as straightness. Having your schooling sessions recorded on video will also help you in assessing your posture and in relating what you are doing in the saddle to how your horse is responding.

Inadequate Preparation

Lack of training, fitness, skipping steps in an exercise, or not establishing each one sufficiently before advancing to the next, can all cause your horse to struggle in his work. Warming up properly at the beginning of exercise is also important psychologically, as well as for optimum physical performance.

Poor Handling

Just because a horse is large or lacks education or experience does not mean you have to be physically assertive: rough, inconsiderate or

Check the horse for any white marks, which can be a sign of damage. This older horse has bony changes in the hocks, and white hairs around the joints are clearly visible.

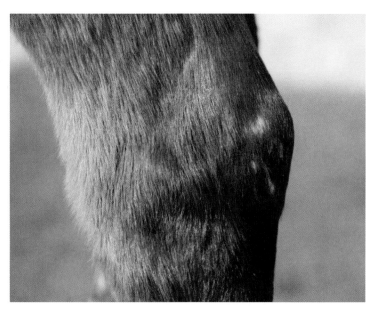

abrupt handling won't teach him to be more obedient or to respect you. It will, however, cause him to become anxious, apprehensive and/or defensive, and make him more difficult to handle or ride.

Training Methods

It can be very easy to fall into the habit of being confrontational and forceful – horses are, on the whole, fairly compliant and easily intimidated, and 'Make him do it' and 'Don't let him get away with it' is frequently heard advice. If your horse is struggling to do something, you should be questioning why this should be, not telling him off for being resistant and bullying him through the difficulty. Training methods should always promote a spirit of confidence and mutual trust.

Be wary of any training aids or riding style which creates exaggerated or forced, unnatural movement and posture: these have no place in equitation and can cause great discomfort and soreness as well as psychological distress.

Poor Communication

Good communication is essential to ensure that your horse understands what is required of him; and he should be invited to comply with your wishes rather than being placed under physical and psychological duress to do so. Your actions need to be calm, clear and without threat.

Communication is, of course, a two-way process; it's not just about letting your horse know what you want him to do, but about listening to him too, and taking note of his responses. Take nothing for granted and never make assumptions – remember that behaviour is not fixed – and try to keep looking at your horse with a fresh eye. Because humans tend to rely more on verbal than body language, we often miss vital cues; time spent simply observing horses and improving our ability to interpret them is never time wasted, and will enable us to spot when he is struggling with anything, whether work related or environmental, and to take steps to deal with it.

PROPRIOCEPTION EXERCISE

1. Hold both hands out in front of you at shoulder height and parallel to the ground, with the palms facing inwards towards each other and around 12in (30cm) apart.
2. Close both your eyes. Slowly raise your right hand up about 45 degrees; keep it in that position and slowly lower the left hand by 45 degrees.
3. Keeping both eyes shut, slowly lower your right hand until you think it is once more horizontal at shoulder height. Raise your left hand so it is once again also at its original starting point.
4. Now open your eyes and look at your hands – it's likely you will find that they are not quite aligned with each other, but that one is higher.

TOP: *You can test your own body awareness with this simple exercise. Start by standing with your feet shoulder-width apart and hold your arms out straight so that they are parallel.*

BOTTOM LEFT: *Close your eyes and raise one arm and lower the other.*

BOTTOM RIGHT: *Keep your eyes closed, and lower and raise your arms until you think they are parallel once more. Open your eyes and see how good your proprioceptive sense is.*

This sweet horse was pulled into a trailer by a chain that was tied round the upper part of his neck and attached to a tractor. The damage to the neck is evident by the presence of white lines at the top of the neck, the dull eye and the lolling tongue.

4 Reading the Horse's Body Language

As well as adopting an open-minded and flexible approach, learning to read a horse's body language will help you to analyse behaviours and decide on appropriate strategies to use while working through any issues with your horse.

READ YOUR HORSE

Your horse's body language provides essential information as to what he is feeling and thinking, and being able to interpret it will increase your empathy and ability to predict his responses, so you are better equipped to make the right choices and take the right actions. Although some people are naturally more observant than others, learning to read your horse is a skill that anybody can learn with patience and practice. Watch your horse – and those of others – at every opportunity, whether in the stable, being worked or interacting with field companions, to build up your visual 'vocabulary'.

The more obvious body language such as kicking and biting, pinning the ears and so on, are well known, but the majority of horses use more subtle body language to communicate with each other and with us. Noticing early signs of concern will minimize the chances of the horse having to become more expressive in his language.

Some horses are easy to read and others more difficult: a horse's ability to be clear in his body language will be determined by several factors. Those which have been hand reared or raised without the company of other youngsters as they start to mature may give conflicting messages as they may not have learnt the necessary equine social skills. Others may have been punished for expressing discomfort, for example being smacked or shouted at for pinning the ears, nipping, air biting or lifting a leg when girthed or rugged up; it stands to reason that the horse will then become more volatile in his communication if his quieter language is punished or ignored. If consistently admonished for attempts to convey that he has a problem, a horse may lose trust in his ability to communicate and may shut down (*see* the section on the eyes, below).

Hormone imbalances, including problems with the pituitary gland, may also change the way in which the horse expresses himself. Although he might appear to be enjoying contact on the upper part of the neck or shoulder because his ears are forward, he may in fact be aroused by this contact and strike without much warning.

Black horses can also be harder to read because it's easy to miss more subtle signs of tension in the body due to their colour – but noting the appearance of the eyes and ears, and the position and movement of the neck and tail, will still give you plenty of useful information.

The Head

Observing your horse's eyes, ears, mouth and

nostrils can provide valuable insights – spend some time studying his head to see if he is evenly muscled around the forehead, whether his protruding cheek bones are similar on both sides, and so on. Dental problems can change the way he is muscled through the jaw and around the skull, while some horses may be born with facial anomalies, or they may have had an accident at some point in their lives which can affect the appearance of the head and face.

The Eyes

The conformation of the eye is instrumental in how your horse processes visual stimulus, but it can also give you an insight as to how he is feeling. Traditionally a large, round, bright, kind eye is considered to be the sign of an easy horse, but shape and appearance can be influenced by many factors. An almond-shaped eye, for example, is often linked with a horse that is perhaps labelled as 'ungenerous' – but because pain and stress will often result in narrowing of the eye (as it does in humans and other animals), the shape of the eye may not be due to conformation alone, but to discomfort on a physical and emotional level. Once the underlying causes for the anxiety are addressed, the eye will often change shape and appearance.

Wrinkles around the eyes and puffy lids can also be a sign that something is amiss. Watch for changes in the colouring of the

membrane around the lower lid and any tension that may be present or starting to become apparent. You may notice the small muscles around the lower lid flickering, or the lower lid may droop, giving the eye a more triangular shape. Pay attention to any hardening of the eye, as this is often one of the first signs of anxiety – always remember that the eye never lies.

A dull eye is a sign that a horse is unwell,

Red coloration around the eye can be a sign of arousal, stress or ill-health.

EXERCISE – JOWL RELEASE

This Connected Riding exercise helps horses to release through the upper part of the neck. It is very subtle, but of benefit to horses that are habitually crooked and/or hang on one rein. Many horses find this exercise difficult at first, particularly if they have worked above or behind the vertical for some time. As well as freeing up your horse it can help you to assess whether he has the ability to release and move his head evenly on both sides.

1. Stand on the right side of the horse's head, facing the side of his jowl. Place your right hand lightly on the nasal bone over the headcollar noseband to steady the head.

2. Make a loose fist with your left hand and place it in the centre of the horse's cheek. Keep your wrist straight to maintain an even connection with your horse, and make sure that you aren't standing too close to him. Stand in balance, with hips and knees slightly and softly flexed.

Support the horse's head by placing the outside hand on the nasal bone. Make a soft fist with the other hand and place the knuckles in the middle of the cheek. Rotate your inside hip slightly towards the horse, which will encourage him to release through the upper part of the neck and the head, as the movement will bring the head slightly towards you. Keep the range of movement small and do not force the horse to flex.

3. Start by pausing to allow your horse to become accustomed to having your hands on his head. If he is happy for you to be handling him in this way, continue with the exercise: the right hand gently invites the horse's head slightly towards you, at the same time as your left hand gently suggests that the cheek move slightly away from you. The movements are really minimal, and you shouldn't see any gross flexion as you don't want to force or twist the nose around towards you – it really is a subtle suggestion as opposed to an obvious movement. Take care not to exert any downward pressure on the nose, either.

4. Maintain this position, and pause for a moment to see if the horse begins to soften and release through the poll. If he is enjoying this exercise you should note

You may notice that the horse starts to clear his nostrils when you work round the head and upper part of the neck.

a softening in his eye; he may also sigh and/or slowly lick and chew. Release the pressure on his cheek and soften the contact on his nose very, very slowly, and wait again to see if he softens and releases during the pause. By rotating your pelvis slowly to the right, then pausing before rotating slowly back to the left, you will encourage him to release even more through the neck, and prevent tension from building up in your own shoulders and arms.

Repeat the exercise, and remember to do it from both sides. You may notice that your horse shakes his head, yawns, or has a nasal discharge after this exercise.

or has shut down and is in a state of 'learned helplessness'. This can occur when he has been consistently punished for expressing himself and has given up, or is worked constantly in ill-fitting equipment, or is ridden by a rider with poor balance who hangs on his mouth and bounces around in the saddle. A horse with a dull eye may appear to be aloof and moody, but this will be linked to his underlying problems and concerns. He may be malnourished, be in constant discomfort, or have been subjected to all manner of abuse in his past.

If you have taken on, or are working with, a horse with a dull eye, be extremely careful. While seemingly quiet and easy to handle, he may reach a point where he simply cannot cope any more, and explodes. He may also feel safe enough in your company to start expressing himself once more. Many novice horse owners unwittingly take on horses like this – but if your 'quiet' horse begins to change, get help straight away. He is not taking advantage of your lack of knowledge – he has a problem.

The Ears

The horse uses his ears for communication as well as to gain information about his surroundings. Their conformation varies from one individual to another: some horses have large, almost floppy ears, whilst others have shorter ears that are generally more erect. Ears that point together are often indicative of a horse considered to be 'hotter' in temperament than a horse whose ear tips are more upright – though this is only a guide, and not something irrefutable.

The ears can provide useful information about a horse's ability to work evenly on both reins, as tension in them indicates tension through the jaw, the neck and the back. Horses that have significant tension around the base of the ear will also often be tighter in the corresponding shoulder, which will result in restriction of

movement in that fore limb. Some horses are so tight through one side of the jaw and neck that they can only move one ear, and apart from the related physical issues, this may affect their ability to communicate. Unlevel ears can be linked to physical problems in the upper part of the neck, and some gentle physiotherapy to address any imbalance may be necessary if they are habitually like this.

Some horses that have been raised without the company of others may give conflicting signals with their ears, so do not rely solely on the position of the ears when attempting to read your horse: as with all body language, look at them within the context of the whole of his body. Having said that, the ears can still provide a lot of useful feedback about how your horse is processing what you are asking him to do.

Pinning the ears back is often used as a warning, and may be accompanied by more volatile body language such as kicking or threatening with the mouth – but many will half pin their ears in a variety of situations, and this is not always an indicator of escalating stress. It may simply be that the horse is processing information, and other body language should be taken into consideration.

Ears forward with a bright expression in the eye would generally indicate that a horse is happy or showing interest in what you are doing with him, while a horse which carries his head high and moves both ears around is listening to sounds you may not be aware of. It can indicate concern in the horse and he may be reluctant to move forwards, or if you are working with him in the stable he may find it hard to settle.

Tension in the upper part of the neck can affect the ability to prick the ears, making the horse appear moody and aloof. Cold ear tips are common in horses that are overly emotional and worried, as well as being an indication of their temperature; this type of horse may also be sensitive to contact on or around the ears.

The Mouth

The mouth is a part of the horse's anatomy that is often inadvertently ignored or misunderstood when attempting to influence and understand behaviour. Licking and chewing is not always a sign that a horse is relaxing – it can also be a sign of escalating stress.

As with the eyes, the shape and appearance of the mouth can give valuable information about your horse's emotional and physical wellbeing – tension around the muzzle, and mouth movements including yawning and nipping, or more subtle signals such as wrinkling the lips, will be indicative of anxiety and/or discomfort.

A tight chin may be accompanied by tight, wrinkled lips, and the horse may be reluctant to open his mouth for the bit, or struggle when given an oral paste wormer. A horse which consistently exhibits these facial characteristics is likely to be more sensitive and emotional than a horse with a more relaxed mouth, and may lack focus and have a short concentration span as a result. He may also be clingy with other horses, reluctant to leave the safety of the yard, and inclined to work with his head in the air.

A horse with a naturally flat chin may flap his lower lip when worried, and this often subtle sign is easily overlooked. When a horse is relaxing, the lower lip will often droop, but if it is perpetually hanging, he is not necessarily in a state of constant calm: it can be indicative of tension in the upper part of the neck, and is often accompanied by a dull eye. Over-bitting, inappropriate use of a pressure head collar, pulling back when tied, a fall, physical problems in the mouth, neck and back and so on can all result in a floppy lower lip. These horses can

be dangerous to handle and ride as they may be prone to bolting or rearing without much warning. Sadly they are often simply labelled as unpredictable without much thought given as to the underlying motives – but as with all behaviours, there will be a reason.

Attention should also be paid to the tongue. Some horses are tense in the tongue as a result of incorrect bitting, because of tension in the muscles around the head and upper part of the neck, or because they have dental problems; or the tongue may have been damaged or twisted at some point in the past.

If the tongue is inhibited in any way it is likely that the horse will be in a habitually incorrect posture. He may be tense in the chest muscles

Some horses suffer accidents or have their tongues tied down which causes damage to the tongue, giving rise to problems with bitting and performance.

and find it hard to lift through the withers. He may also appear to be a picky eater and will lose weight easily, as he may struggle to eat food such as hay, which requires him to use his tongue to manoeuvre it in his mouth. Ensure that he has access to good quality grass if possible, and supplement his diet with regular feeds of chaff during the rehabilitation process. A horse with restricted movement through the tongue will also tend to be dry mouthed when ridden.

TTouch Mouth Work (*see* Exercise 'Mouth Work') can have a dramatic and positive effect on both confidence and concentration, as well as addressing any concerns that your horse may have about being handled around the mouth. It will also have a profound influence on how your horse processes information and, together with other exercises that help to free up the entire body, will enhance all aspects of his life.

The Nostrils

The shape of the nostrils will vary slightly from one horse to another, but like the eyes and ears, can provide a lot of information about how the individual feels. Tight, narrow nostrils are often present in horses that appear to lack tolerance, but this is rarely just a temperament or conformation issue, and is usually linked to other difficulties that the horse may be experiencing – once the underlying problems have been addressed, the nostrils often change shape.

The height of your horse's nostrils may change during the day, but if you notice that one nostril is permanently higher than the other, you will probably also note that the position of the ears is uneven too. Whilst nothing in nature is symmetrical, unlevel nostrils and ears usually indicate problems in the first two cervical vertebrae in the upper part of the neck. This can generally be corrected by body-work exercises such as TTEAM, physiotherapy or McTimoney Chiropractic.

THE IMPORTANCE OF BODY POSTURE

Not many people are aware of the importance of the horse's posture when it comes to behaviour, but the two are inextricably linked. It's likely that you have subconsciously witnessed it in humans though: a person feeling happy and confident will literally be walking tall with a spring in their step, while someone feeling anxious or depressed may adopt a hunched posture and drag their feet.

Just as emotions can affect posture, so posture can influence feelings and attitude for better or worse. Developing a more correct carriage doesn't just enable more efficient body use and relieve physical discomfort caused by poor posture, but it can produce a more positive mindset.

Changing posture can, however, only help influence behaviour for the better if it is managed correctly. A horse in a high-headed frame is often more highly strung than a horse that is moving correctly through the body with a lower head carriage. Teaching him to lower his head on cue may therefore be useful, but only if he is relaxed through his whole body and able to breathe rhythmically and deeply by releasing along the whole of his top line and opening the ribs. If he remains braced through the neck and back, then standing with his head low will have very little beneficial effect on the nervous system. Enforcing a lowered head carriage by pulling him into a false outline with training equipment or a strong hand can actually have an adverse effect as the tension created through the neck and body can trigger spooking and a host of other unwanted behaviours.

It is really important to pay attention to the posture of the horse at all times, whether you are grooming him, working him in hand or simply bringing him in from the field. If he is frightened or unsure at any point he will raise his head, drop his back and lose connection with his hindquarters. This is not the posture that we want in the ridden horse, so be careful about inadvertently reinforcing this inappropriate posture when handling your horse.

Muscle memory plays an important part of any work, and it is increased through movement. It is therefore important to 'teach' the horse's body how to work effectively so that a correct posture is established which allows for optimum balance and power. It is alarming how quickly a horse can develop incorrect muscle through the back and neck and therefore the rest of the body; just one hour in a badly fitting saddle, for example, will have a dramatic impact on the horse even if he spends the remaining twenty-three hours grazing in a field with his head down and his top line lengthened. On the positive side, provided any contributory factors are addressed, correct muscle can be developed just as fast if work in hand and body-work exercises to speed up the learning process are also employed.

As a rider you will have to work on your own muscle memory as well so that you can address any of your own postural habits that may be impeding the performance of the horse. The more attention you pay to detail regarding your own posture as well as that of your horse, the easier it will become.

Tension Patterns

Any areas of tension which exist in the body due to physical, emotional or environmental

Stroke your horse slowly all over his body with the flat of your hand and watch for any signs of ticklishness or tension. Pay attention to how your horse responds, and do not punish him if he pulls faces, attempts to bite, or raises a hind leg. He is merely trying to tell you that he has a problem.

stresses will not only have a knock-on effect on posture generally, but can lead to specific behaviours. Many horses will use the area where tension occurs to express themselves: a horse that bites or grabs the lead line or your clothing is often tight in the mouth and through the hinge point of the jaw; a horse that kicks is often tense around the hindquarters, tail and down the hamstrings; and a horse that bucks will usually have tension through the lumbar area, reduced mobility through the hocks, and/ or tension around the girth area.

As well as identifying areas of tension through observation, use your sense of touch, too: starting at the poll, run your hands over every single part of your horse's body on both sides, noting any peculiarities; these might include:

● Changes of body temperature: a horse prone to spooking, for example, may have cold lower legs and cold areas over the nasal bone and hindquarters, whilst the presence of heat in the body will generally be indicative of inflammation
● Coat texture: note variations including raised or staring patches, dullness, curly or thinning hairs, greasiness or scurfiness, or areas where the coat may have been rubbed away due to ill-fitting equipment or as a result of a poor posture that has left rub marks on each side of the neck from the reins
● Lumps and bumps
● Spasming of skin or muscle when a certain area is touched
● A tight feeling in the skin or underlying muscle tissue
● Whether your horse pulls faces or tries to move away to avoid contact, or expresses his concern in any way
● Ticklish areas, as these are usually linked to tension in, or near, the sensitive spots
● White hairs around the hocks, poll, base of the neck and so on will indicate areas of tension and discomfort, or where damage has occurred in the past

With experience it is possible to ascertain how a horse is likely to perform and behave simply by looking at the way he is muscled and where any tension patterns exist – even the way in which the mane falls can tell you a lot. The correlation between posture and behaviour is a fascinating subject, and study of it can reap great rewards, but it is too large a topic to do more than touch on briefly here. If you want to explore it further, you will find suggestions for further reading in the information section at the end of this book.

LEARN TO LISTEN

Use your ears in addition to your eyes and sense of touch to help you assess your horse and identify problem areas. As well as vocalizations such as snorting when anxious or nickering as a greeting, listen for other noises he might make, such as gulping and sighing. Frequent gulping can be a sign of stress, and a thorough veterinary examination to investigate the function of the digestive system and any other sources of discomfort should be considered. Slow, deep sighing as the horse lowers his head and softens his eye can be a sign of relaxation, but frequent shallow sighing can be linked to tension through the back and withers.

Pay attention to the sound of his footfall, too, or any creaking or clicking as he moves. Pain is a contributory factor to many behavioural problems: if one hoof hits the ground with more of a thud than the others, or the gait rhythm is irregular, your horse is unlevel and may even be lame. Note whether he scuffs the ground with the front or hind toes or just one toe, which again will be indicative of an uneven gait. Whilst potential problems with the limbs must of course be ruled out, movement of the fore- and hindquarters will also be influenced by the neck and the back.

5 Establishing a Problem-Free Relationship

It is important to consider what sort of relationship you want with your horse when working with him, and that you understand the impact of everything you do.

There are many ways to train a horse: some methods rely on confrontational and coercive practices, while others use aversive techniques that make him uncomfortable when behaving inappropriately, with his 'reward' being the cessation of the discomfort when he behaves or moves in a way that is deemed acceptable.

REWARD-BASED TRAINING

We believe it is kinder and far more successful, both in the short and the long term, to use techniques that focus instead on what the horse can do, rather than on what he can't, techniques that offer more positive forms of reward, and that teach him how to use his body more efficiently and to behave in the way we want by setting him up to be successful.

Over and over again we have heard it said that the owner/handler/rider should always 'come out on top' – but if this is your priority, both you and your horse will lose out. Whilst it is necessary to set boundaries, and to be consistent with those boundaries, it is far better to work towards a partnership based on harmony, understanding and trust: this in itself will be rewarding for you and your horse. Movement should be rewarding too, and your horse should feel good after hacking, schooling or working in hand. He may be tired, but he should not be overly fatigued, and he should certainly not feel sore. This rule also applies to you as a rider, and if you suffer from back pain, sore shoulders or legs after riding, something is amiss. You may need help with your own posture, your saddle may need attention, or your horse may be working or muscled up incorrectly.

Offering Rewards

Recognizing even a small improvement, and rewarding it, is important, as it lets your horse know that he has done something well, and will help motivate him to repeat the action. Rewards can take different forms, whether it is a word of praise, stroking or scratching his neck, shoulders or withers, offering a treat, allowing him a chance to stretch on a long rein, or even stopping work for the day.

Your horse needs to be rewarded as soon as possible after the action you wanted has occurred if he is to make an association between the two. When working towards a particular goal, chunking actions down into smaller, easily attainable steps not only makes it easier for your horse to be successful and to grow in confidence, but it provides you with plenty of opportunities to reward him and give him encouragement.

TELLINGTON TTOUCH

We make no excuse for wholeheartedly recommending Tellington TTouch – also known as TTEAM – as a really useful teaching tool for all occasions, and one that can be invaluable when faced with challenging situations. A small-scale but fascinating study conducted at Bitsa Olympic Centre in Russia showed conclusively that after TTouch body work was performed, horses' levels of stress hormones were reduced, their behaviour was calmer, their movement and capacity for work were improved, and bad habits were more effectively resolved.

Tellington TTouch is a kind and respectful way of working with horses to help them overcome a variety of health and behavioural issues. It was developed over thirty years ago by Linda Tellington Jones, and is now widely used around the world by trainers, riders, vets, physiotherapists, riding instructors, and people working with welfare organizations.

The technique recognizes an inextricable link between posture and behaviour, and uses body work, ground-work exercises, ridden exercises and specific equipment to release tension and to promote a feeling of calm and wellbeing. This in turn helps horses develop self-confidence and self-control, and enables them to move beyond their instinctive, and often fearful, responses.

Contrary to outdated beliefs, handling a fearful, defensive or reactive animal in a positive, mindful and calm way does not reward (and therefore reinforce) that behaviour: it can change it. Tellington TTouch has a profound and potent effect on the nervous system, and a powerful influence on responses and mood. Even well established patterns of behaviour often alter within a very short space of time, and Tellington TTouch has saved the lives of many horses whose behaviour was deemed to be out of control, as well as enhancing the lives of many more.

Body Work

The body TTouches consist of a variety of specific light pressure touches which aim to increase mind/body awareness and to give the horse new information and experiences by engaging the sensory aspect of the nervous system. They are highly beneficial in helping an animal to release muscle tension around a specific joint or body part, in reducing stress and improving spatial awareness. Many of the TTouches are named after the animals that originally inspired them – and this is also a fun way of remembering them.

The position of the hand, and the pressure and the type of TTouch used, will vary from horse to horse, and will depend on the horse's responses to contact and the part of the body that is being TTouched. For example, nervous and defensive animals usually find contact with the back of the hand far less threatening, and may initially only be able to tolerate being TTouched on their shoulder.

Circular TTouch Exercises

The circular TTouches are the foundation of the TTouch body-work technique and can be used over all the body. The fingers or hand actually move the horse's skin gently in one and a quarter circles, usually in a clockwise direction, although some horses prefer anti-clockwise circles. The pressure is light, and most people find this hard to comprehend as they think they must work deep into the muscle in order to be effective, which is untrue.

When you are ready to start working on a horse, you may find he is more accepting of contact on specific parts of his body. Most horses find TTouches on their shoulders more acceptable, so this may be a useful place to start. Start on the left side of your horse as you will probably find this easier, holding the lead line with your left hand whilst you do the TTouches with the right

EXERCISE: CLOUDED LEOPARD TTOUCH

1. You can practise this circular TTouch on yourself: first, rest your fingertips gently on your other arm with the first pads of your fingers making contact with your skin. Rest the thumb on your arm for support. Imagine a watch-face on the skin: your fingers will be at the six.

2. Keeping your fingers in contact with the same piece of skin, gently push the skin in a circular movement around the imaginary watch-face, passing through all the numbers from six, nine, twelve, three and six. Continue on past the starting point until you reach eight so that you start and end the circular TTouch by guiding the tissue in an upward direction.

The Clouded Leopard TTouch can be done anywhere on the body. Keep the hand soft, and gently move the skin in one and a quarter circles with your fingertips.

3. Pay attention to the shape of the circle, and keep your hand soft. You should notice that your wrist and finger joints move as well. If you brace your hand and reduce the movement through your fingers the pressure will be increased and less comfortable. Remember to breathe and keep the movement slow. It should ideally take around three to four seconds for you to push the skin around the imaginary watch-face. You only need enough pressure to move the skin, and you should notice that your finger tips create a slight indentation in your arm.

4. Once you have completed one circular movement, slide your fingers to another part of your arm and repeat the movement. Try moving the skin in both a clockwise and anti-clockwise direction. Most people find that the tissue moves more easily in one direction than the other.

EXERCISE: LYING LEOPARD TTOUCH

This is a slightly 'softer' TTouch than the Clouded Leopard. The principles and movement are the same, but the hand is flattened slightly so that the first and second parts of your fingers are in contact with the body. Experiment with both TTouches to see which one your horse prefers, or use both to give him a different experience.

EXERCISE: LLAMA TTOUCH

If your horse is extremely sensitive and/or nervous, turn your hand over so that the contact is made with the back of your fingers and/or hand. This is a useful way to initiate contact with a fearful horse, and will help you to refine your skills as you cannot inadvertently apply too much pressure with this TTouch.

Use the Llama TTouch for sensitive areas such as round the muzzle or if the horse is nervous. Some horses find contact with the back of the fingers or hand more acceptable.

one. Stand by his neck and rest your hand on his shoulder. Keep your arm and wrist straight, as flexion in the wrist will increase the pressure, which is not the aim. You will obviously need to move as you work on his shoulder, up his neck and along his back: gently slide your fingers to another area after each circular TTouch, and pay attention to his body language at all times. If he seems restless, try speeding up the movement initially, and/or doing random TTouches rather than sliding your hand to another part of his body. If he remains unsure, try a different TTouch.

OTHER TTOUCHES

You will find many other TTouches described in this book which you might like to try, including Ear Work, Tail Work, Mouth Work, Jellyfish Jiggles, Forelock Circles and Slides, Forelock Pulls, Sternum Lifts, Wither Rocking, Leg Circles, and Lick of the Cow's Tongue (*see* Key to Exercises). You will find details of how to learn more about other TTouches in the Further Information section.

Ground Work

Leading the horse through patterns of poles laid on the ground, over low raised boards, through cones and over different textured surfaces helps to improve his proprioception, focus and balance.

The slow, precise movements of the ground-work exercises help horses to settle, and to learn the ability to self calm. They also increase flexibility and improve correct gait locomotion. Physical, emotional and mental balance are all linked, and ground-work exercises can have a dramatic effect on behaviour; they are particularly useful for horses on reduced exercise, or for those that become over-excited when ridden. They can also be a valuable starting point for horses that cannot tolerate physical contact, a problem usually indicative of pain, expectation of pain, or high levels of tension present in the body.

Ridden Work

Ridden exercises build on the exercises that are taught from the ground. Body-work exercises can also be used during ridden work if working with a partner, enabling horse and rider to experience together the freedom of movement that both may be keen to achieve.

Equipment

TTouch practitioners use specific equipment for both ground-work and ridden exercises, such as a 'wand' to help cue actions, or the Balance Rein and the body wrap to help engage the hindquarters, encourage the horse to lift through the withers, and lengthen and ultimately strengthen the back.

Body Wraps

Body wraps are exercises which improve proprioception and therefore gait, help an anxious horse to settle, encourage hind-limb engagement, promote relaxation, and improve mind/body awareness. Many horse owners and riders worldwide are astounded at the profound effects of these simple training tools, which have helped numerous horses overcome both health and behavioural difficulties.

EXERCISE: THE HALF WRAP

You will need two 10cm- (4in-) wide wraps for a horse, or two 8cm- (3in-) wide wraps for a pony.

Start by tying one wrap around the chest and shoulders, as explained below and shown in the photo. This is called a 'Base Wrap', and is the cornerstone of all the body wraps. Most horses accept this relatively quickly, but if a horse has issues with rugs or has previously had problems with a breastplate, it may have a negative association with anything that goes around this part of the body.

1. Stand on the left side of the horse. Keeping hold of one end of the wrap in your left hand, carefully unroll it and pass the remainder of the wrap under the neck and up to the right hand at the base of the

TOP: The Base Wrap is tied round the base of the horse's neck and is the cornerstone of all the body wraps. Horses that are braced in the neck, are high headed, or work consistently on the forehand will benefit from this wrap. Once the horse is happy with the wrap you can tie it in a knot or bow to keep it secure.

MIDDLE: Tie one wrap round the base of the neck and attach the second wrap on the off side. Bring the wrap under the horse round the girth area, and attach the end to the base wrap with a quick release knot.

BOTTOM: The Half Wrap is beneficial for horses that rush, lean on the forehand, or have poor balance and co-ordination. It is also a useful stepping stone when starting or re-starting horses under saddle, and for those that have girthing issues, and it can also be helpful for horses that are worried about wearing rugs.

neck, above the withers. Tie the ends together with a quick release knot, and draw it back slightly so it lies across the back just behind the withers. Make sure the knot doesn't rest against any bony areas such as the top of the shoulder or the withers.

2. Lead the horse around the yard or arena so that he becomes accustomed to the feel of the wrap. You may notice that he slows his pace if he has a tendency to rush, or starts to lower his neck and head. If he is happy with this Base Wrap, you can ask a helper to tie a second wrap to it on the right-hand side of the horse by the top of his shoulder. Ask them to pass the remainder of the wrap to you behind the elbow and beneath the horse, and then bring the wrap up on your side so that it lies around the girth area. Attach it to the Base Wrap with a quick release knot. It should be a close but not a tight fit. Be careful if the horse is sensitive in the girth area and/or cold backed, has issues with being saddled or rugged, or has never worn anything on the body before. In such instances, or if you have any concerns that your horse may not tolerate the Half Wrap, teach the Belly Lifts exercise (*see* Key to Exercises) first.

EXERCISE: THE FULL WRAP

There are two ways that you can make a Full Wrap: the Bridge Wrap and the Figure-Eight Wrap. The choice will be determined largely by the conformation of your horse, and partly by what you want to achieve. We recommend using the Bridge Wrap after you have tried the Half Wrap, and before you try the Figure-Eight Wrap, which may be preferable for horses with rounded withers or sloping hindquarters.

Depending on the size of your horse, you will need two or three 10cm- (4in-) wide Ace wraps.

The Bridge Wrap

The Bridge Wrap is best used as the introductory Full Wrap as it attaches to the Base Wrap around the neck. If the second wrap slips down too far, try the Figure Eight Wrap instead.

1. Ask a helper to tie one end of the second wrap in the same way as when applying the Half Wrap, but this time pass the end of it over the top of your horse's back to you. Make sure you don't drop it or allow it to flap around in the wind. Tie your end to the Base Wrap by the top of the shoulder on your side, being sure to use quick release knots on both sides.

2. Ask your helper to hold the horse, standing on the same side as you while you carefully slide the bandage over the hindquarters so that it is positioned half way between the point of the buttocks and the gaskin. The front part will form a 'bridge' of bandage passing over the horse's back just behind the withers. Place the rear part of the wrap over the top of the tail until you are sure of his response to it, so it is easier to remove if he shows any anxiety about it. The wrap should fit closely enough that it maintains contact with the body and does not slip down the quarters, but should not be tight. Do not use this wrap if there is any risk of being

kicked. Watch your horse's body language at all times: even if he is used to fillet strings or leg straps he may be concerned by the sensation of the body wrap. If he is worried at any point, stop.

When he first moves forward he may rush for a few steps, as the feeling of engagement may unsettle him. Most horses quieten quickly with this wrap, although some may cover the ground more powerfully and effortlessly – so be prepared! Remember, if he is really concerned about it, remove the wrap and ask your vet to check him over, as he may have a physical problem.

The Figure-Eight Wrap

1. Ask someone to hold the horse. Tie all the wraps together to make one long bandage, and then re-roll them. Standing on the left side of your horse, unroll a short length, and pass it around the base of the neck and hold it at the withers.
2. Hold the shorter end in your left hand, and uncurl the rest of the wrap with your right one, crossing it over in an X just behind the wither, and tying the ends together with a quick release knot so you have a figure-eight shape. Slide the large loop of the lower part of the figure eight around the hindquarters, ensuring that the knots lie against soft tissue and not on top of the spine. The wrap should be a close, but not a tight fit.

The Figure-Eight Wrap is one of the Full Wraps used to encourage hind-limb engagement and improve balance and co-ordination.

We recommend that you purchase 'Ace' wraps which are available from the TTEAM UK office and also abroad (*see* the Further Information section at the end of this book). If you cannot locate an Ace wrap, elasticated exercise bandages may be used instead, but make sure they are long enough, as the aim of the wrap is to increase awareness and not restrict movement in any way. Wrapping the head and/or neck of the horse can be useful for helping horses that are pushy with their heads, lose focus, are crooked in the neck, or carry tension through the forehead and neck. Wraps can also be used to improve awareness of one or more of the limbs.

There are many ways to use a wrap on the body of the horse; the two main ones are the Half Wrap and the Full Wrap (*see* sidebar). The Half Wrap can be useful for horses that rush and find it hard to stand still, because it helps in rebalancing a horse which is on the forehand; it can also be a useful preliminary step in introducing a surcingle and/or a girth. It can be used while doing all the ground-work exercises. The Full Wrap has many beneficial applications, in particular with horses that rush, find it hard to stand in balance, have gait irregularities, lack hind-limb engagement, stumble, spook, are worried about narrow spaces, or are reluctant loaders.

There are many other ways in which wraps can be used; for those who would like more information we suggest buying the TTEAM booklet *All Wrapped Up for Horses* by Robyn Hood (*see* the Further Information section at the end of this book).

CONNECTED RIDING

As well as many TTEAM exercises there are some Connected Riding exercises included in this book. One of the authors – Sarah – has worked with Peggy Cummings, who in addition to being a TTEAM practitioner, has developed her own system of body-work, ground-work and ridden exercises based on thirty years of equine experience.

Peggy spends much of her time travelling and teaching, and we recommend attending a Connected Riding event if you can. She also has practitioners in Canada, the USA and Europe. Her exercises are aimed at improving the horse's performance not just by addressing areas of bracing and/or tension whilst improving the connection through the horse's body, but by helping the rider improve their own posture through finding what Peggy calls a 'neutral pelvis'. This enables all riders to find true balance, and not only helps the horse to move more freely and correctly, but ensures that the rider is also free from pain and tension, regardless of their age or level of experience.

This principle of 'neutral pelvis' is also used in Peggy's ground-work exercises, and has a dramatic and powerful influence on the efficacy of this work for both horse and handler. Furthermore, learning how to move and ride in 'neutral pelvis' enables both horse and rider to develop core strength – and core strength is integral to balance, stamina and fluid movement: in other words, everything that we are looking for in the ridden horse.

CLICKER TRAINING

As horses – like most animals – learn by association and work on a 'motive and reward' basis, clicker training can be a brilliant way to work with a horse. There is no end to the fun you can have with the clicker; it is relatively easy to learn and will give you new insights into how a horse moves, thinks and learns, as well as deepening the bond between you.

You can use it to change a horse's expectation of something he finds difficult, to improve performance, or simply to give him necessary mental stimulation if you are limited in the time that you spend with him. With horses that cannot be ridden due to physical and/or behavioural concerns, clicker training can be the perfect tool for owners who wish to maintain a relationship with their horse when other activities are no longer viable.

A clicker is a small plastic mechanical device that clicks when the metal strip is depressed by the thumb. The click serves as a 'yes' to the horse, and a small piece of food is given following the click to encourage the horse to repeat the behaviour that triggered the click. Food is a primary motivator, and thus is the quickest way to encourage the horse to repeat or build on a specific behaviour. You can purchase clickers that are relatively quiet, but if a horse is worried by the noise, pick a word which you don't use in everyday life with him, and use this word in place of the click to mark the behaviour that you would like him to repeat. This also means that you can use this method at times when you need to use both hands, such as when riding.

Clicker training very much focuses on what the horse can do. It is a positive way to train any horse, regardless of his age or breed, and contrary to what some people may think, does not encourage unwanted behaviour around food. As with any training system, there are different methods and thoughts about how to apply clicker training, and you may like to explore these further.

Targeting

The easiest way to start clicker training is to teach the horse to target a plastic lid with his nose. It is best to start this exercise with the horse on the other side of a barrier such as a stable door or a wooden gate, to avoid being mugged for food until he understands what is being asked of him. It will also enable you to watch his reactions from a safe position. Ensure that he cannot get a hoof stuck in the bars of the gate if he paws the air.

You will need a clicker on a lanyard or a clip that attaches to your pocket so that you don't drop it, and a variety of treats in a feed bowl or in a bag on a belt around your waist. Some horses will work for hay or grass, whilst others prefer to work for something of higher value such as small pieces of carrot, parsnip, apple or horse treats. The treats need to be small so that you can work consistently without waiting for the horse to munch large quantities.

Always keep sessions short, as you want the horse to be keen to work, but not to get overly excited or to lose interest. Several short sessions are far better than one long one in any training that you do, and it is often during the breaks that the horse truly processes what he was learning.

Taking It Further

Teaching your horse to target something on a verbal cue can have many practical applications: thus by varying the position of the lid you can encourage him to flex to left and right, move back, or lower his head to lengthen his topline. You can progress to attaching the lid to different parts of the stable wall so that he also learns to move away from you and stand next to a target on cue. You can also encourage him to follow a moving target, which will then give you a good foundation when working on the ground or starting the steps to helping him with any loading issues.

If at any point he struggles with the exercise, go back a step. Building a solid foundation is the key to any training, and clicker work is no different.

EXERCISE: CLICKER TARGETING

This exercise can be a good way of introducing clicker training, and this particular exercise can be developed to help with issues such as outline, stiffness and travelling.

1. Stand to one side of the door and hold out for example a supplement lid at nose height and slightly away from you. Your horse's natural curiosity will probably mean that he reaches forwards to touch the lid with his muzzle. The moment he touches the lid, click and give him a treat. Lower the lid each time you give him a treat, and deliver the treat by moving your hand towards him so that he learns to step backwards before taking the treat. Practise this for a few minutes, then give him a little break whilst you do some yard duties.

2. Repeat the exercise again, and if he is confidently touching the lid with his nose the moment you hold out the lid, slightly change its position and/or height. Do not rush him and overface him, otherwise he will lose both confidence and the association with the lid, the clicker and the treat. Patience is the key, and you may also need to work on your timing. Stay calm, and remember that you are learning, too.

3. Build on this exercise over a few days. Some horses take to it really quickly, while others are a little slower to grasp the idea. Clicker training will improve your horse's ability to think and learn, so even if he starts slowly, don't give up! Once he has learned not to mug you for food, and that the treat only comes following the click, you can work in his stable with him – though make sure that the food is kept in a pocket or in a bag around your waist. If at any point he begins to mug you or gets pushy, simply walk away.

Hold out a plastic lid in front of the horse and the moment he touches it with his nose, click and give him a treat. Start by having a barrier between you and the horse in case he mugs you for the food until he learns that he only receives a treat after he has heard the click.

Once he has grasped the concept, move the lid, but if he struggles go back to the earlier step.

4. Remember that the clicker marks the behaviour you would like him to repeat, so only click when he touches the lid with his muzzle; if, for example, he opens his mouth, or touches you instead, simply don't click and treat. It's also important to remain quiet so you don't distract him with your voice. Once you know that every time you hold out the lid he will touch it without fail with his nose, you can add a word cue such as 'Touch'.

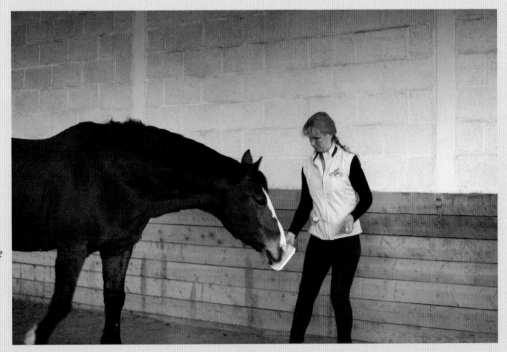

Progress to working inside the stable or barn with the horse and teach him to walk towards the target.

RECORD KEEPING

Keeping a notebook can be a good way of keeping track of progress: visual records in the form of photographs and video can also be invaluable in helping you to analyse movement, behaviour and interactions, and in pinpointing possible causes.

CALMING SUPPLEMENTS AND DRUGS

A thriving market in various 'calming' supplements and additives exists, but think carefully before using them. In some cases they can be useful in helping the horse to cope while the underlying causes of unwanted behaviours are being remedied, but they should not be viewed as a quick fix or a substitute for putting in the necessary work with your horse.

Bear in mind that just because a product is described as 'natural' it does not necessarily mean it is safe: some may create imbalances, and the effect can be variable between individuals. If you compete, you should also be aware that some substances may be prohibited if your horse is drug tested.

VISUALIZATION

Visualization may seem fanciful to some, but don't scoff until you've tried it. It has been acknowledged for years by neuro linguistic programming (NLP) practitioners as being a powerful tool which helps you to replace negative thoughts with positive mental images. This can make a tremendous difference to your outlook and approach to resolving problems, as well as to the way in which you respond to a horse, and the situations you find yourself in. It is a subject which is a whole book in itself – *see* the Further Information section.

KEY POINTS FOR A SUCCESSFUL STRATEGY

Whatever the undesirable behaviour you want to change, there are certain key points which you should always keep in mind.

Deal with the Underlying Causes

When a problem arises, an often heard response is 'He's never done anything like that before'. Maybe not, but the chances are that it's been brewing for a period of time before that. Problems rarely occur out of thin air for no reason at all, and just because you can't immediately identify a reason for the behaviour, it doesn't mean that one doesn't exist. Although the behaviour itself may need to be addressed, if you don't also seek to remedy any underlying causes (there may be several), it may be difficult to make any progress, and whatever you do achieve is likely to be short-lived. Like taking aspirin to relieve the pain of toothache, if the tooth itself remains untreated, sooner or later trouble will bubble up again.

Avoid Force

Using bullying, intimidating or forceful tactics to deal with a problem can make it worse, and may lead to other, more dangerous behaviours developing; such tactics will also destroy trust and confidence. Results achieved through working in a quiet way, with the horse being given the opportunity and encouragement to want to participate in the learning process, are likely to be safer, less stressful, and therefore more successful, and will also probably last longer.

Make Solutions Simple

Don't make things harder than they need be. Chunk exercises down into small, progressive steps, and master each stage before moving to the next one.

Tailor your Approach

Adapt your approach to the individual horse. No two horses are the same, and the right solution for one may not be appropriate for another, even if it exhibits a similar behaviour.

Be Flexible

Although it's good to have a goal, you also need to be flexible, as things don't always go according to plan. If a horse is struggling with an exercise, or to do anything you are asking him to do, think about how you can make it easier for him. You may have progressed too quickly, worked for too long, the horse may have a problem that inhibits his learning, or you may need to try a different exercise.

Be Consistent

It is important to be able to follow consistently the strategy you have decided upon – and if you can't manage the work on a regular basis, you may need to rethink and devise a more feasible plan.

Be Patient

Don't expect instant results – sometimes you may see beneficial changes very quickly, but in many cases resolving difficulties takes time and patience. Be realistic about what and how much you can achieve during each session and within a given period of time. Generally, the longer a problem has persisted, the longer it will take to change it.

Remember to stay focused on what you have achieved, not on what you haven't: this is another occasion when keeping a training diary is helpful, as it can be easier to see the progress you have made.

End Lessons on a Good Note

Ending a lesson on a good note is always the ideal, but this doesn't mean you have to see what you started through to completion within that session. Return to a familiar and less challenging exercise which is easily within your horse's ability to achieve, or stop the session completely and give him a break so as not to sap his physical reserves or damage his confidence.

If you have had to stop because he was struggling and becoming difficult to handle, go back a few steps and keep the next session short and fun. This will help you to move forwards more quickly than if you try to battle on.

Take Appropriate Safety Precautions

People often underestimate the danger they place themselves in, but if you are casual or complacent about your own safety, you may well take risks with that of others, and of the horse, too.

When working with any horse, be sure to choose an area that is safely enclosed and surfaced, and be conscious of the welfare of those assisting you. Always wear suitable clothing and footwear yourself when handling or riding horses. Wear a hard hat, with the chin strap fastened – not just when riding, but also when working with a horse from the ground, particularly if there is any likelihood of it being reactive. Gloves are sensible for hand protection when leading, and a body protector is advisable if riding any horse that is likely to be unpredictable in its actions.

Acquire the Right Tools

Before you start working with your horse, make sure you have the tools you will need at your disposal, whether physical aids, skills or knowledge. Know your own limitations as well as abilities, and seek help in those areas where you lack expertise.

PART 3
A–Z DIRECTORY OF PROBLEMS

INTRODUCTION

The issues covered in this section are the most common of those which affect horses and riders/handlers. Although we are not enthusiastic about applying labels to behaviours for the reasons explained in Part 2, we have nevertheless retained the traditional terminology because it is necessary to have some way of identifying various issues. But try not to let these names fix you in your way of thinking – some solutions may require a bit of lateral thinking: in tackling one behaviour, you may also find there are other related issues, or even that what you initially thought to be the primary problem is actually a side effect of something else entirely.

Please remember that every horse is an individual, and every situation is different. Although there may be certain commonly shared factors, it is really important not to adopt a 'one size fits all' approach to problem solving: what is appropriate and highly successful for one horse may not be right for another. The causes and solutions offered here are not the only ones, but are suggestions designed to give you a place to start; in many cases you may need to adopt a variety of resources rather than applying a single technique or procedure.

Furthermore, many behaviours are interlinked, so you will find that many of the headings here refer you to others. Although the connections between some may not always seem immediately apparent, there are often shared factors, so do read each of the additional references, even if at first glance you don't think they apply. And if you haven't already done so, we also suggest that you read the first two sections, as understanding the background to behaviours is crucial to resolving them.

Always study closely the horse you are working with, and let him guide you. Good observation will help you in making the right choices – by noting any improvements you will know when you are on the right track, and to desist if what you are doing is making matters worse.

In all your work, removing any source of conflict, pain or other underlying cause of a problem is always central to resolving any difficulties, as is building and retaining mutual trust and respect between you and the horse. Sometimes there are quick fixes, but more often than not you will need to exercise patience, and be committed to a longer term strategy if you want to achieve a lasting result, and avoid damaging your relationship with the horse.

DIRECTORY OF PROBLEMS

Note that at the end of each of the problems in the following directory the reader is referred to exercises that might be helpful in resolving that problem. To find these cross-referred exercises quickly and easily, the reader should go to the Key to Exercises at the beginning of this book: this Key contains an alphabetical list of all the exercises given in this book, and the name of the problem in whose text it will be found (the problems in this directory are also listed alphabetically).

For example, at the end of the problem 'Aggression' (*see* below), it is suggested that the reader might try the exercise 'Wand Work' as being helpful in resolving that problem: to find this exercise, locate it in the alphabetical list in the Key to Exercises, see which problem it is contained in ('Wand Work' will be found in the problem 'Grooming issues'), then locate that problem in the A–Z directory below.

AGGRESSION
See also Balance, Bullying, Cowkicking, Kicking, Mareish behaviour.

'Aggression' is a classic example of an often misleading label – moreover it can also produce a very negative mindset which may then be reflected in the way the horse is handled. Behaviours such as biting and kicking are more often than not defensive actions due to fear and pain, rather than to a horse being 'nasty'.

The chances are that the horse may already have been giving clear warning signs, such as pulling a face, laying his ears back, shaking his head, air snapping or lifting a foot in response to discomfort caused by, for example, rough handling. If these are ignored or dismissed as 'naughtiness', the behaviour becomes more extreme in an attempt to make the handler desist, and a bite or kick threat can develop into a realized and frightening behaviour which can result in serious injury.

In some cases the horse may exhibit actions which appear aggressive as a way of discouraging you from approaching because of anticipation of discomfort. Irritability and intolerance can also be caused by pain due to ailment or injury – discomfort can make the sweetest tempered of horses less than tractable and often downright grumpy.

The handler's instinctive reaction is to shout at and/or smack the horse when it presents threatening behaviour, but retaliation may provoke an even more violent response and only increases the horse's anticipation of unpleasantness. Tying the horse up short while handling him may stop him from being able to reach you with his teeth, but if you fail to deal with the cause of his anxiety or discomfort he may swing his quarters towards you instead, and strike out with his forefeet or cowkick instead. Don't rule out the possibility that although such behaviours may occur from poor or insensitive handling, they can also be due to unpleasant associations with being ridden.

Competition for food may also lead to perceived 'aggressive' behaviour; for this reason it is advisable not to feed concentrate rations to horses that are loose in the field, and if you take food with you to catch a horse which is out with others, keep it in your hand or pocket rather

than in a bucket so you do not inadvertently get caught up in the middle of a fight over it. Always leave your horse to eat in peace and quiet, and when stabled, avoid placing the feed bucket next to the partition between stables.

Other horses passing by a stable may sometimes generate a bite threat from the occupant, often due to insecurity and fear. A stabled horse has nowhere to retreat to, and threatening behaviour to discourage any approach may be the only way he has of creating distance between himself and others. If a horse is suffering from mobility problems, this behaviour may also occur for similar reasons, as the ability to move quickly and easily away from any sources of concern will be impaired.

For the safety of others, as well as to reduce levels of concern, horses which are likely to threaten passers-by or to bite over the stable door should be stabled where they are not subjected to constant traffic from horses or people going past.

Suggested exercise: Wand Work

BALANCE, LACK OF EMOTIONAL
See also Balance, lack of physical

For many years now it has been recognized that a direct link exists between posture, emotions and behaviour – and just as feelings can influence posture for better or worse, so the reverse is true. Author Aldous Huxley, a student of the Alexander Technique (a modality which helps teach correct postural alignment and balance), commented: 'If you teach an individual first to be aware of his physical organization, and then to use it as it was meant to be used, you can often change his entire attitude to life and cure his neurotic tendencies' – a truth acknowledged by many other modalities including chiropractic, yoga, Feldenkrais and Tellington TTouch.

Balance is always a critical factor in a horse's ability to do anything, and a horse which is

EXERCISE: STERNUM LIFTS

This exercise helps to teach your horse how to transfer his weight backwards off his forehand; although he may find it hard to achieve much movement initially, if practised over several days you will begin to notice a definite difference.

1. Stand just in advance of, and to one side of your horse's shoulders, and facing towards his quarters. Place the palm of the hand closest to your horse on his chest, between his forelegs and positioned on the sternum (breastbone). Space your feet comfortably apart, with the one closest to your horse placed slightly further forward than the other, and with the knee and hip joints slightly flexed.

2. Ask your horse to transfer his weight back off his forehand by using your bodyweight to initiate and maintain the movement. Do this by slowly adjusting your posture so that your centre of gravity gradually rocks forwards over the leg closest to your horse. At the same time as the pressure of your hand against his chest increases, think of it lifting diagonally upwards too, following the angle of his shoulders towards the wither.

3. Hold for a moment, and then slowly release the lift by gradually moving your centre of gravity back again over your rear foot. Repeat two or three times.

Imagine a diagonal line passing from your hand, between the shoulders and up to the withers. Lean into the movement so that it comes from your own body and not just your arm and gently push upwards, hold for a moment and then slowly release maintaining the contact on the chest. Some horses are sensitive around the chest and others are so tight you will not see any movement initially.

Place the palm of your inside hand in the middle of the horse's chest, just in front of the front limbs.

physically in balance will not only be able to cope better with the athletic demands made of him, but will be in a better mental equilibrium too. Even small improvements in posture can produce a huge difference in his temperament and his ability to learn and progress, which will make handling and riding him easier and safer, as well as making life more pleasant for the horse himself.

Suggested exercises: Body Wraps, Labyrinth, Mouth Work, Stroking the Line, Tail Work, ZigZag

BALANCE, LACK OF PHYSICAL
See also Balance, on the forehand, Clumsiness, Crookedness, Outline, Standing still, Stumbling, Tying up

A physically well balanced horse will be safer to ride and handle, better able to do what is asked of him and emotionally more stable, and will find it easier to take the unexpected in his stride. Balance is something which most people usually associate with the horse when in movement, but lack of it can also be a major cause of problems when standing still, whether under saddle, in hand or when tied up.

Good balance isn't something which happens all at once, but is achieved over a period of time through the use of various ground-work, ridden and body-work exercises that help to develop core strength, self-awareness and co-ordination. Half halts, transition work and riding accurate school figures can all be invaluable in improving balance under saddle.

Care should be taken not to rush the training process or to hurry the horse out of his natural gait as this will result in poor balance, as will an incorrect, or incorrectly achieved outline. Similarly, a horse which is very one-sided will find it difficult to be in balance. Look closely at the way in which he is muscled; while nothing in nature is symmetrical, many horses are more unbalanced through the body than they should be due to asymmetrical muscular development.

Poor conformation will affect the horse's ability to balance too, as can health issues; age can be another factor, with stiff joints creating difficulties for older horses, and growth spurts changing perceptions and co-ordination in young ones. Rider positional faults such as leaning forwards, backwards or sitting crookedly will also have a major influence on the horse's balance, and will need help from someone on the ground to correct.

Suggested exercises: Balance Rein, Forelock Pulls, Labyrinth, Leg Circles, Sternum Lifts, Tail Work, Tracing the Arc, Wither Rocking

BALANCE, ON THE FOREHAND
See also Balance, lack of physical, Clumsiness, Outline, Stumbling

A horse's natural balance tends to be with 60 per cent of his bodyweight supported over the forehand, but this unequal weight distribution not only puts increased strain on the front legs, but can create difficulties when riding. The horse will tend to work 'downhill', will lack the ability to use his quarters efficiently, and will be more likely to stumble and tire quickly. Upward and downward transitions will be difficult for him to achieve, and he may find it difficult to stand still for any length of time.

Judicious and careful use of half halts, transitions and lateral movements during ridden work will be helpful; introducing the Balance Rein is also a very effective way of teaching him how to transfer his weight backwards correctly, and can be taught from the ground as well as used while riding. With horses that tend to lean on the rider's hands, overbend, or which are high headed, it will also help produce a better quality of rein contact and an improved outline.

EXERCISE: USING THE BALANCE REIN

Introduce the Balance Rein from the ground in a safe, enclosed area. If you don't have a TTEAM Balance Rein as shown here, use a 2m (7ft) length of 13mm (½in) wide climbing rope, or improvise with an old leadrope, cutting the clip off first.

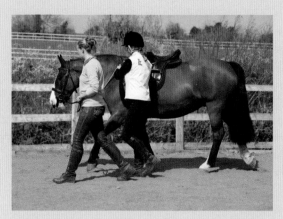

1. Ask someone to lead your horse while you walk alongside holding one end of the rope in each hand, allowing it to hang loosely round the underside of the horse's neck.

2. When you want to halt, give a gentle signal on the Balance Rein in an upward and diagonal direction following the line of the horse's shoulder. Avoid pulling it sideways, as this may cause a lateral loss of balance.

Place the Balance Rein round the neck, unbuckled. Hold it in the inside hand in front of the withers, holding the other end with the outside hand. Ask a helper to lead your horse forwards in walk for a few steps, keeping the Balance Rein slack.

3. Immediately after giving the signal, release the tension so the Balance Rein hangs slack again; it is on the 'release' that your horse will slow, or stop. Keeping up a constant pull will encourage him to lean against it. If you find he doesn't take any notice, try a slightly firmer ask-and-release signal, and if necessary your assistant can also cue him. With patience and practice you'll find that eventually you can halt using the Balance Rein alone.

4. Once you are reliably achieving a halt without needing assistance from your helper, you are ready to move on to ridden work. Secure the ends of the Balance Rein so it forms a complete loop, and place it round your horse's neck so it lies beneath the bridle reins. Hold the bridle reins as usual, and the Balance Rein so it passes between the second and third fingers of each hand. Ask your assistant to continue walking alongside initially, in case you need help, because if you aren't used to holding two pairs of reins you may find that it feels awkward at first. Check that the Balance Rein isn't too long; if it is, you'll find yourself holding your hands too high or pulling them backwards, which can put you off balance and make your signals crude, unclear and unco-ordinated.

After a few steps, give an upwards ask-and-release signal on the Balance Rein, keeping it in line with the front of the shoulder blade. Use your voice to give the signal to whoa, and remember to ask and then release, as it is on the release that the horse will stop. You may need to ask your helper to back up the cue to stop at the beginning, but most horses learn this really quickly.

5. Ride your horse forwards in walk, keeping the Balance Rein slack; after a few steps ask him to stop by using the 'ask-and-release' signal on the Balance Rein as before. Ride plenty of transitions between walk and halt in this way; each time your horse will be learning how to lighten his forehand, improving his balance and ability to stop promptly, correctly and efficiently. You should also find his stride becoming longer, and that he is moving with more freedom through the shoulders and greater engagement of the hindquarters.

6. Once the walk and halt work is established, introduce trot and then canter. You can also begin to use the Balance Rein in more subtle ways to help influence balance while in movement as well as during transitions.

Once the horse is comfortable working in hand, progress to using the Balance Rein under saddle. Remember to use an ask-and-release signal to slow or halt the horse. Tina is holding the balance rein in one hand to help this young cob, Myrtle, balance through the turn, but you can also hold it in two hands to take pressure off the bit.

Suggested exercises: Balance Rein, Clicker Targeting, Floating Forwards, Neutral Pelvis, Raised Polework, Solo Polework, Sternum Lifts

BARGING
See also Balance, lack of physical, Crowding, Doors, Escaping, from stable, Leading

BEDDING, DIGGING UP
See also Stereotypies

Disturbed bedding can indicate restlessness – due to box walking perhaps, or colic, or if the horse has become cast. If the bedding is piled up to make higher and lower areas it may be an attempt to relieve some kind of physical discomfort such as laminitis, back problems or soreness in the pelvic region.

Suggested exercises: Belly Lifts, Ear Work, Lick of the Cow's Tongue, Tail Work

BEDDING, EATING
See also Coprophagia, Pica

Eating bedding may be due to hunger or boredom, or a combination of the two. In some cases it can lead to digestive upset, as well as leaving the horse with insufficient covering on the floor, which may make him reluctant to urinate or to lie down. Replacing the bedding with a less palatable alternative such as paper, woodchips or hemp may deter him, but doesn't get to the root of the problem.

Ensure the horse is provided with sufficient forage to satisfy both appetite and the innate desire to graze; if weight considerations are a factor, rather than limiting the bulk fibre intake, soak the hay for twelve hours to reduce its calorific value.

Using a ground-level slow feeder is another way of helping to keep a bored horse occupied and slowing down greedy ones; several types are available in the US – although not, unfortunately, in the UK at present. A search on the internet will, however, produce details of various ways to make a home-made version.

Suggested exercises: Belly Lifts, Ear Work, Mouth Work, Tail Work

BIT EVASIONS
See also Balance, Bolting, Crookedness, High-headed, Jogging, Outline, Pulling, Rearing

There are many ways a horse can evade or resist the action of the bit; these might include raising his head, opening his mouth, crossing his jaw, chewing excessively, grinding his teeth, placing his tongue over the bit, leaning against the contact, overbending, tossing his head, and snatching the reins away from the rider.

Most of these behaviours are an indication of discomfort, and in such instances using a tight noseband to close the mouth or some gadget to hold the headcarriage steady is inhumane; the reason why the horse is seeking to avoid the contact should always be sought out and remedied. The causes can be numerous, but start by asking your vet or an equine dental technician to examine the teeth. They will have a special piece of equipment called a Hausmans gag, which is used to keep the mouth open, and will be used to check the teeth thoroughly and safely – so this is not a job you can do yourself.

The type of bit, and the mouthpiece width and diameter, may also be responsible for the problem: it may be unsuitable for the horse's mouth size and conformation, or over severe, too narrow, too wide or hanging too high or low. Check also that the browband is not too short and pulling the headpiece forward into the sensitive area at the base of the ears, as this can cause behaviours which may be misinterpreted as being due to the bit. An over-tight throatlash can also make it difficult for the horse to flex and accept the bit.

Headcarriage, lack of balance, longitudinal and lateral stiffness and incorrect musculature will all affect the way a horse moves and therefore the quality of the rein contact, so it may be necessary also to look at ways of bringing him into a better balance and increasing suppleness throughout his body.

Poor rein management by the rider may also be responsible for creating pain in the horse's mouth, which he will understandably seek to avoid: working to establish an independent, balanced position in the saddle should be an ongoing commitment. It is also important not to use the reins to manipulate the horse into an outline – a busy, nagging hand will produce a distorted outline and is often responsible for bit evasions.

Suggested exercises: Balance Rein, Body Wraps, Ear Work, Floating Forwards, Forelock Pulls, Mouth Work, Neutral Pelvis, Promise Wrap, Reverse Reins, Sternum Lifts, Stroking the Reins, Tail Work, Tracing the Arc

BITING
See Aggression, Bullying

BITING, AT REINS
See Aggression, Chewing

BOLTING, FEED
See Eating

BOLTING, WHILE RIDDEN
See also Balance, Bit evasions, Pulling, Rearing

A bolting horse is a danger to himself, his rider and others; in an extreme state of fear and panic, he takes no notice of the rider, and if something gets in his way there is a possibility that he will go over or through it, or headlong into it.

Horses which exhibit such behaviour are often found to be clamped in their tails, and with tension present in the ears and upper part of the neck. They may have bony changes in the hock, or be unable to lift through the back. Pain, or a frightening incident such as a bird scarer going off nearby, may set the horse off, but not all triggers may be obvious to you.

EXERCISE: REVERSE REINS

Hold the reins so they pass from the horse's mouth through the top of your hands between your thumb and first finger. Keep your hands angled so that your thumbs point along the reins towards the horse's mouth. For safety, only try this while working in an enclosed area, and if necessary ask someone to lead the horse from his noseband. This riding exercise will create a more passive, softer rein contact: holding your reins in this way makes it impossible to fiddle the head into an outline, encourages you to carry the hand towards the horse rather than restricting him, makes it difficult for you to use the reins for support or to pull on, and will give both you and your horse a different but pleasant experience.

This exercise will make it very difficult for you to be forceful with the rein contact, and will increase your awareness of any reliance on it for balance. Make sure you angle your hands so that wrists, forearms and reins all form a straight line with the horse's mouth.

Horses have more acute senses of smell and hearing than we do, and the unseen can hold just as many fears for them as visible objects.

As with rearing, there is often a pattern to the behaviour, although it isn't always easy to spot and you may need to look much further back for its origins than the events immediately preceding him bolting. Find the pattern and then hopefully you can identify the contributory causes and work on them as appropriate.

A horse which gets very strong, as opposed to the genuine bolter, can be just as frightening and dangerous, and is sometimes nearly as hard to stop. It can be due to a number of reasons, including over-excitement when cantering in company, anticipation of cantering or galloping, over-feeding of concentrates, a combination of over-confinement and lack of exercise, poor riding, pain caused by the rider or saddlery, or a physical problem (mouth and back problems are often linked), lack of schooling, poor balance, insecurity and lack of confidence. Most horses will also tend to speed up when heading towards home, and this can sometimes get out of hand.

Safety must always be paramount: do not 'over-horse' yourself, and avoid putting your horse in a situation where he is likely to become out of control. Spend time working at home on improving balance and responsiveness to the aids, and on developing confidence and trust so he is less likely to be spooked into a panic reaction. As a short-term strategy, use saddlery appropriate to your activities – your horse may be fine in a mild snaffle while working in the school, but may need a running martingale or slightly stronger bit when hacking out. Care should be taken in the selection – always try out anything new at home in a safely enclosed area, and bear in mind that if bitting is too severe or the rider employs it too roughly it may have the opposite effect to that intended: the horse may panic and fight it, pulling more strongly, or draw its head in behind the vertical, dropping behind the contact. Teaching your horse the Balance Rein exercise can be very helpful, and is a good way of 'nipping things in the bud' if your horse begins to get a little strong in your hand, without having to resort to stronger rein aids.

EXERCISE: WORK OVER DIFFERENT SURFACES

Many horses are concerned about crossing white road markings, passing drain covers and so on, while some loading issues are actually linked to the horse's reluctance to walk on to a ramp that may be covered in matting rather than to the prospect of actually being in a lorry or trailer, so this simple exercise is an important one for many reasons.

As well as increasing levels of self-confidence, teaching your horse to work over different surfaces encourages more efficient brain–body use, improves hoof–eye co-ordination, and develops self control, so it can be a great way of preparing him for anything you might encounter when out on a ride or at a show.

Teach this work first from the ground and in a safe environment that the horse already knows before repeating it under saddle. Showing your horse how to do the exercise and making him do it are two totally different things, and he should not be forced to walk over the surfaces at any point. By being patient, taking your time

Walking horses over different surfaces helps them to become more confident and improves their proprioceptive sense. It also improves focus and self-control, and helps horses to become less concerned about novel situations. Build slowly so that the horse is not overfaced, and incorporate them into the ground-work sessions with poles.

and really listening to your horse, you can usually teach him to walk over a variety of objects quietly and safely in one or two sessions, and even horses that are habitually spooky can usually learn to walk calmly over a variety of surfaces in a relatively short space of time.

1. Begin by teaching your horse to walk through the Labyrinth or double Zigzag, asking him to halt at various points as he moves through the poles.
2. Once he is confident with either or both of those exercises, place a carpet mat, rubber car mat or a sheet of wood with a non-slip surface in between the poles. Start with a single piece initially, making sure that the surface you have chosen is large enough for him to walk on to with his front feet, but not too wide in case he panics and tries to jump it. Also ensure that he cannot tip the surface when he treads on it, or catch it with a hoof, as this will alarm him, and that it is solid enough for him to walk on without it cracking.

3. Walk him up to the surface and ask him to halt a few strides before it. Let him look at it, and if he is really concerned, simply turn him away. Lead him around the surface by walking over and parallel to the poles, but avoid forcing him to walk close to it if he is really anxious.

4. If he is able to halt, ask him to continue on over the surface, but note the speed with which he does so: if he rushes and cannot stop on the other side of the surface his anxiety levels are high. Some horses are more worried by the noise that the surface makes, so if you have decided to use some wood, walk over it yourself while leading your horse next to the surface so that he becomes accustomed to the noise before stepping on to it himself.

5. Repeat the exercise a few times every day or even a couple of times a day, approaching the surface from different directions. Incorporate it into other leading exercises if you have the time so that the focus is not simply on the different surfaces. Some horses find it easier to walk between the poles, while others find it easier to walk over a pole on to the surface, and then out over a second pole – so try not to be rigid in your approach.

6. Once the horse is able to walk calmly up to, then on to the surface, and halt calmly on the other side of it, ask him to stop with his front or back feet on it. Add other, different surfaces one at a time, but keep the surface he is familiar with as the first one you approach. Starting with something he has already learned will give him the confidence to try new things.

Suggested exercises: Balance Rein, Body Wraps, Caterpillar, Ear Work, Leg Circles, Mouth Work, Neck Rock, Raised Poles, Solo Polework, Stroking the Line, Tail Work, Wand Work, Work Over Different Surfaces

BOX WALKING
See Stereotypies

BRIDLE, DIFFICULT TO
See also Bit evasions, Catching, Head shy

Horses anxious about having their heads handled are also likely to be difficult about having the bridle put on. Time should be spent rebuilding confidence in having the head and ears touched (*see* Head shy), as well as checking for any signs of physical discomfort, in particular with regard to the teeth, mouth or ears, or from the effects of trauma of some sort, especially in the poll area.

The bridle should be a good fit – often the browband is too short, so that the headpiece is pulled into the base of the ears – and correctly adjusted so that the bit lies at the right height in the mouth. The bit itself should be an appropriate size for the conformation of the mouth, and with no sharp edges or joints which pinch. Sometimes unpleasant associations between the bridle and work are formed, and this is certainly a factor worth considering.

Many horses suffer from clumsy bridling. For example, if the horse's front teeth are knocked every time the bit is put into his mouth, a lack of co-operation is understandable. Bridling a tall horse can be difficult if you are short, especially if he puts his head in the air, so encourage the horse to lower his head for you by offering a food treat, and as he does so, slip the reins over his head and neck so you can keep him from wandering off. If he is reluctant to lower his head for food, use the headpiece of the bridle to make a loop with which you can capture his nose and then draw it down towards you: reward him with the treat if he will take it. You could also use the clicker target exercise to teach him to lower his head.

Stand facing forwards on his near (left)

side, bring your right hand under his jaw and around the front of his nose, and hold both the cheekpieces in it while offering the bit with the left hand. If he tries to raise his head you can gently but firmly prevent him from doing so with your right hand: and as the bit slips into his mouth raise the bridle cheekpieces held in your right hand so it doesn't drop down and bang the front teeth. As well as giving you more control, putting the bridle on like this is less alarming for your horse: it is also safer for you than facing towards him, when you could get hit in the face by his nose or the bridle if he suddenly throws his head up.

If the horse clamps his jaws shut and won't open his mouth to take the bit, use a treat to encourage him, or place the thumb of your left hand into the side of his mouth in the gap between the front and back teeth and exert a slight downward pressure on the tongue. If he is very anxious about his teeth being banged, use a non-metal or covered bit until he is more confident about being bridled.

Some horses are reluctant to open their mouth and allow the bit to drop out when the bridle is taken off, and if the bit becomes hooked behind the front teeth this can cause a horse to panic. Try using a similar technique as when bridling, to help control the height of the horse's head and keep the bit supported, and food to encourage him to open his mouth. If you find this awkward to manage, offer some food in a bowl on the ground: as his head goes down, take the headpiece over his ears and allow the bit to drop out as he takes a mouthful.

Suggested exercises: Caterpillar, Clicker, Ear Work, Forelock Circles and Slides, Forelock Pulls, Jowl Release, Mouth Work, Stroking the Line, Tail Work

BUCKING
See Girth issues, Jumping, Saddling issues

Bucking when turned out in the field is usually due to high spirits; it may also occur while working if the horse is under-exercised and/or overfed, and not receiving sufficient turnout. Generally it happens early on in the work programme, and is usually an expression of frustration at being restricted rather than due to over-exuberance; sometimes it also happens when galloping in a group, which can trigger instinctive behaviours. Flies can be another cause of occasional bucking: horseflies and gadflies both have a painful bite, and the presence of the latter can send some horses into a frenzy.

A horse that bucks regularly while under saddle or working in hand usually does so because it is in pain, and this certainly needs to be investigated. Back problems are common in horses, but while this may spring to mind first as a reason for bucking, pain elsewhere in the body may also account for this behaviour: this might be tension around the girth area, hormonal issues in mares, kidney problems, a dirty sheath, or discomfort created by the saddle, girth, a crupper, the rider, or incorrect use of the whip.

Bucking is also an instinctive behaviour which may happen at moments of fear – it is an action designed to dislodge an attacking predator or to discourage one in pursuit. Take time and care at every stage of training with young, nervous and inexperienced horses when introducing them to a potentially frightening/threatening experience, such as wearing a saddle or rug, being girthed up, or having a rider sitting on them. Observe them closely, because although they may appear to be coping well, this may not be the case, and if there is any underlying anxiety it may surface explosively when you are least expecting it. It can be useful to perform ground- and body-work exercises such as Walking the S and Tail Work before mounting, as they will help the horse to relax by encouraging the release

EXERCISE: FORELOCK CIRCLES AND SLIDES

This is a great exercise for reducing a horse's concern over the bridle and headcollar; it starts by releasing tension from the ears and poll, and helps to relax the forehead and the hinge point for the jaw. It is simple to do, and something which the majority of horses enjoy. Forelock Circles and Slides can also be done when the horse is bridled to help him relax before the rider mounts.

1. Stand in front and slightly to one side of your horse. Rest one hand lightly on the noseband of the headcollar or bridle, keeping the fingers open and without tightening your grip around it – then if your horse flings his head up, your fingers will slide off easily. Using the other hand, gently take a strand of the forelock and stroke the hair lightly from the base right out to the end. The aim is to relax the horse and to release tension from between the ears, the forehead and around the forelock and poll, so ensure that you work slowly and calmly. Work the entire forelock in this manner. Watch to see if there is movement through the skin around the forelock – if the horse carries a lot of tension here there may be minimal movement through this area at first, but it should increase as the horse begins to relax.

2. Once your horse is happy with Forelock Slides, take the forelock in your hand close to its roots, and gently and slowly circle it in both clockwise and anticlockwise directions. Note whether the horse prefers a particular direction, and watch his eye and ear set for any signs of concern.

TOP: *Support the head by gently resting your fingers on the noseband. Avoid gripping the noseband in case the horse throws his head up in the air. Hold the forelock with the other hand and circle the hair slowly in both directions.*

MIDDLE: *Forelock circles help to release tension through the upper part of the neck and around the head, and most horses really enjoy the sensation. If your horse is concerned try the forelock slides initially.*

LEFT: *Forelock slides can be done before mounting to help the horse soften and relax through the jaw, head and neck. Gently stroke the forelock from the base to the tip. If the horse has a thick mane you can stroke the forelock in sections.*

EXERCISE: WALKING THE S

Even if you don't have any specific problems, this is a useful warming-up exercise before starting work, as it will help loosen up lateral stiffness and release tension in the neck and rib cage.

1. Standing next to your horse, lightly hold the bridle noseband with the fingers of the hand closest to him.
2. Lead him through a series of shallow S-shaped loops, keeping your knees, hips and back soft, and arm joints flexed and supple. Rotate your body a little to the right to help guide your horse through the right-handed loops, and to the left through the left-handed ones, rather than pushing and pulling with your arms.

ABOVE: *This exercise can be done when walking out to, or in from the field; it can also be done when the horse is saddled prior to mounting. Support the head by resting the inside hand on the noseband and rotate your body away from the horse as you walk which will naturally draw the horse towards you. Pay attention to any resistance that you feel as this will have a direct correlation with how the horse moves under saddle.*

3. Walk four or five strides in each loop. Keep them fairly shallow at first, gradually increasing the depth as your horse begins to find them easier.

LEFT: *Rotate your body in the other direction and make sure that you are in balance yourself. Avoid pushing the horse's head, and keep the movement as smooth as possible. The aim is to walk the horse in a shallow serpentine, and not pull him or push him around.*

of tension held in the back and through the ribs.

Suggested exercises: Belly Lifts, Body Wrap, Lick of the Cow's Tongue, Tail Work, Walking the S

BULLYING
See also Aggression

Overstocked fields can lead to bullying, usually primarily because of competition for food, but also partly because it is harder for individuals to maintain their personal space. If putting hay out when grazing is scarce, always put out at least one more pile than the number of horses – and preferably more – and space them well apart. Bickering may also break out if you go to catch your horse and very obviously have food, and are seen to be handing it out.

Mixed sex grazing can often lead to problems too, especially when mares come into season, and also if the members of the group are constantly changing with different horses coming and going. Introducing any new horse to an established group may cause disruption to the herd dynamics, but the process of integration can be made smoother and safer if it is done gradually. Working the horses together in the school and riding out together will help, and, if possible, turn out the new horse in an adjacent paddock initially; for safety the dividing fencing should be post and rail, not wire, and ideally double fenced with a gap between the two.

Once the newcomer has had a chance to settle, it can sometimes be helpful to turn one of the other horses out with him so they can buddy up together, so that when he finally goes out with the group he already has one friend. When the time comes to do this, put boots on them all (provided your horse is accustomed to them), with tape over the top of the fastenings to keep them secure, and keep an eye on the group until you are sure they are all settled. We also recommend removing the back shoes, if this is viable.

Occasionally a horse will be picked on to the point of injury, and it may become necessary to transfer him to another field with quieter company – or to remove the aggressor if he picks on other horses too. The vet should be asked to check the aggressor over for any health issues which may be at the root of the behaviour. Where a horse is habitually being picked on, health problems may also be responsible, whether because of the way he moves, his appearance, or even something as subtle as smelling 'wrong', and he should also be checked over.

Sometimes the situation is not what you first thought, and the horse being bullied may in fact be pestering the other horses until they strike out at him through sheer irritation – so watch them all carefully to see who really is at fault. Although horses are herd animals, some may prefer their own company to that of others, depending on previous experiences and socialization.

Bullying is not a behaviour confined solely to the paddock; it can also happen to horses in adjoining stables, or when they are travelling in a lorry or trailer. As well as raising stress levels generally, it may contribute to the development of unwanted behaviours or reinforce any existing anxieties, so both stable and travel companions should be selected with care.

CANTER, CHANGING LEADS
See also Balance, Canter, disunited, Crookedness, Outline, Stiffness

Persistently changing the canter lead can be due to discomfort from the saddle or bit, or because of pain in the back or elsewhere in the body or limbs; horses that find it difficult to canter on a specific lead will often try to revert to the opposite, more comfortable, one.

Youngsters, stiff horses, those struggling to produce a greater degree of collection than they are ready for, or asked to work deeper into corners or on smaller circles than they are capable of coping with, or at any time when balance is lost or interfered with, will also be likely to change canter leads. This can also be a common problem if you try to advance your horse too quickly in counter canter work.

Sometimes it is a problem of rider position, rather than the horse's problem, caused by the rider sitting crookedly, or by sudden weight, rein or leg aids that interfere with balance, or – in the case of horses that are being taught, or have mastered flying changes – are misunderstood.

The Connected Riding exercise 'Neutral Pelvis'

EXERCISE: NEUTRAL PELVIS

You can find neutral pelvis by sitting on a chair, and then use the same principles once you are in the saddle:

1. Sit near the edge of the chair, feet and knees apart and resting your hands on your thighs or allowing them to hang loosely by your sides. 'Walk' forward on your seat bones a fraction. Try doing a tiny back-and-forth rocking movement with your upper body. How does it feel? Now raise your sternum (the breast bone) a little to create a slight arch in your back. Try rocking slightly forward and back again. Does the tiny movement feel less fluid and not quite as effortless as before? Now drop your sternum so that you slump slightly and try the rocking movement again. How does the movement feel now? Go back to the middle point where the sternum is neither up nor down, and rock slightly forward and back once more. Keep the movement subtle so that anyone watching would be unaware of you moving. This posture should enable you to move effortlessly in perfect balance without the need to push or brace with any other part of the body. Your body

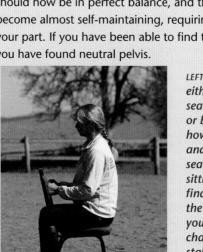

ABOVE: Sit astride on a chair facing backwards and place your fists on the back of the chair. Push the back of the chair and note what happens with your body. If you are sitting on the back of your seat bones your upper body will be pushed backwards, and you'll feel yourself rounding your shoulders and collapsing through the front of your ribcage.

should now be in perfect balance, and the rocking movement will become almost self-maintaining, requiring little, if any, work on your part. If you have been able to find this place on the chair, then you have found neutral pelvis.

ABOVE: If you are sitting on the front of your seat bones your upper body will move forwards, and as you push with your fists, you'll feel yourself stiffening and hollowing your lower back.

LEFT: If you have moved in either direction, 'walk' on your seat bones either forwards or backwards, depending on how your upper body moved, and push on the back of the seat once more. If you are sitting in balance you will find that you sink more into the seat of the chair when you press on the back of the chair and your upper body is stable. This is neutral pelvis. Experiment with this exercise and transfer it to the saddle the next time you ride your horse.

2. Once in the saddle, find neutral pelvis by placing your legs in front of the saddle flaps. You can do this on a saddle horse or while mounted, although ask someone to hold your horse if he is not sure about this movement on his back. Women generally need to walk forward on their seat bones around one eighth of an inch, and men generally need to walk back an eighth of an inch to come into neutral pelvis. Take a piece of the horse's mane, or hold the saddlecloth in front of the saddle, and pull: you should feel that your body is completely stable without having to activate any muscle. If you are pulled forwards, or if you are bracing through the body, you have not found neutral pelvis.

EXERCISE: FLOATING FORWARDS

The energy from the horse's hindquarters and the momentum of the forward movement causes many riders to bring their upper bodies behind the vertical. This leads to a loss of balance, which the rider then compensates for by tightening and bracing in the upper thighs, hips, lower back and shoulders, which in turn restricts movement through the horse's body.

To be able to stay in harmony with the horse's movement, first find neutral pelvis (see the preceding problem), and then as the horse moves off, allow your upper body to float slightly forwards, remembering to let this happen with every stride. Now the motion of the horse will be automatically balancing your body. It is a minute movement forwards, and should not be visible to someone on the ground. This will help you to stay straight and light on the horse's back whilst maintaining equilibrium, allowing him to move freely and effortlessly beneath you.

ABOVE LEFT: **To compensate for the natural drive of the hindquarters you need to find neutral pelvis and imagine that you are slightly leaning into an oncoming wind, and float your upper body forward. This will help you to sit in balance and move with the horse, which in turn will free up his back and increase the length of his stride. Notice the huge difference this change in rider posture makes to that of the horse in these two pictures.**

ABOVE RIGHT: **The movement of the horse can make a rider unstable in the saddle, and many riders sit behind the vertical, pushing the horse forwards with the seat bones, which in turn forces the horse on to its forehand.**

can be life changing for both you and your horse. In essence, the stomach muscles, known as 'core' muscles, enable the human body to stay upright. When the rider is in 'neutral pelvis' these core muscles engage automatically, which helps them to maintain their balance on a horse in any situation, including when it spooks or is nappy, or suddenly jibs and freezes.

Horses are also less likely to evade the aids or brace in their body when the rider is in true balance. Because neutral pelvis enables this true balance to happen, the rider can become much more pro-active – part of the solution instead of unintentionally being part of the problem.

Neutral pelvis can be achieved easily by the majority of riders, regardless of age or experience – and it can be applied in other situations, too. If you are in neutral pelvis when working with your horse from the ground you will be far more effective as a handler, and able to influence your horse's balance more quickly, than if you are braced and inadvertently hanging on to the lead line. Engaging the core muscles will also reduce the chances of you hurting your back when carrying out stable duties.

Suggested exercises: Caterpillar, Floating Forwards, Jowl Release, Lick of the Cow's Tongue, Mouth Work, Neutral Pelvis, Tail Rolling, Tracing the Arc

CANTER, DISUNITED
See also Balance, Canter, changing leads, Crookedness, Stiffness

Whether the horse strikes off into a disunited canter, or becomes disunited while cantering, the causes are similar to those of other canter problems: the horse is in discomfort, and/or he is struggling to cope with the demands made on him. Youngsters or older horses that lack co-ordination and strength may be especially prone to this, so the rider must try to keep the

seat quiet and light, and ask for shorter periods of canter. This problem may also arise when working on flying changes, when the horse may change in front but not behind; in this case it may be due to insufficient engagement of the quarters.

Suggested exercises: Balance Rein, Floating Forwards, Pelvic Rotations, Promise Wrap, Tail Work

CANTER, FAVOURING ONE LEAD
See also Balance, Canter, changing leads, Canter, disunited, Clumsiness, Crookedness, Laziness, Rushing

Favouring one particular canter lead can often be due to extreme one-sidedness, so it can be instructive to look at the horse's quarters to see if one side is more developed in appearance than the other. The first leg to take the canter will be the hind leg diagonally opposite the leading foreleg – so if the right foreleg is leading, the left hind leg will initiate the canter. If the horse has difficulty in taking the right canter lead, it may be due to some difficulty in the locomotion of the left hind leg – and so too in the other diagonal. Where the horse consistently has trouble in taking a particular canter lead, arrange to have him examined by the vet and a physiotherapist; saddle fit should also be checked.

Established habit and incorrect musculature may make it difficult for the horse to take a particular canter lead. Ground work and exercises aimed at encouraging more symmetrical development will help, and the rider will also need to ride accurately and ensure the horse maintains balance.

Try not to let achieving the correct lead become a major issue for you, as it can lead to over-riding and poor posture, making matters even more difficult for your horse. Practise riding transitions at lower gaits, improving activity and responsiveness to the leg aids

EXERCISE: RAISED POLEWORK

When a horse lifts a front leg over a pole, the neck should lower and the withers and back should lift and release, encouraging engagement of the hindquarters. If he is tight through his back and has developed a bottom line through working above the vertical he may struggle to walk over a raised pole at first, and it will be helpful to teach the exercise in hand initially so there is no constriction from the saddle or the rider's weight.

1. Start with four or five poles lying flat on the ground and set parallel to each other. Adjust the distance between the poles to suit the stride of your horse. If possible, ask someone to watch you work, or teach someone how to do the exercise so that you can make observations as to how the horse is organizing himself over the poles, and use the TTEAM lead line and wand as described in the section on leading. If your horse is panicked by poles, start with a single one and build up the exercise over several sessions.

2. Position yourself a little in front of your horse's nose to encourage straightness and even movement through the shoulders. Lead him up to the poles and halt a couple of strides away in front of the first pole. Stroke down his chest and front legs with the wand, then ask him to step forward over the poles with a slight ask-and-release signal on the lead line. Slide your hand down the line away from the headcollar as you do so, to give the horse more freedom through his neck and head as he walks over the poles, and give a forward movement with the wand. Look in the direction you are going, and try to gain feedback about how your horse is organizing his body through the sensations you feel on the lead line. He may hang towards you, or stumble over the poles, or catch one with a hoof. Look for a pattern in his movement as this will relate to any schooling difficulties he may have.

TOP: *Riding over raised poles improves the horse's proprioceptive sense, his focus and co-ordination. This lovely Shire stallion is really paying attention to the poles. Note whether your horse hits the poles with a specific leg or legs.*

BOTTOM: *You can also place the poles in a fan shape to increase co-ordination and flexibility. Start with the poles flat on the ground, then raise the ends at the narrowest point of the fan. Note whether the horse finds it easier to work in one direction than the other.*

3. Once your horse is effortlessly and consistently working over the poles, vary the exercise by raising every other pole, or by raising alternate ends, or raising them all.

4. You can also introduce some flexion into the exercise by arranging the poles into a fan shape. Start with them flat on the ground and see if your horse finds it easier to move in one particular direction. He may find it hard to flex through the ribs or to lengthen the muscles on one side of his body.

5. Once he has mastered this exercise, you can raise the ends of the poles at the point of the fan. This will mean that he has to move his inside legs with a more elevated and shorter step than those on the outside, which can help with gait and co-ordination when working on the flat.

so that this does not become a part of the problem when asking for canter, or lead to him running on to the forehand. Use half halts to balance the horse and activate the hind leg prior to asking for canter, and ask for the transition on a circle or in a corner with a correct flexion to the inside through the length of the spine. Raising the inside hand slightly may be helpful, but avoid drawing it backwards. Sometimes it may be easier to obtain the correct lead by going directly from walk, rather than from trot to canter, as these are both lateral gaits: it can also be easier to maintain both horse and rider posture. Asking for a few steps of shoulder-fore, or positioning the quarters inwards very slightly, may also help – try both in order to find which is of most help in positioning your horse to take the correct lead. If using quarters-in, once you reliably begin to achieve a correct strike-off, start to phase it out to avoid encouraging crookedness.

Another way of encouraging a horse to take the inside canter lead and giving him a feel for the desired locomotion is to place a single pole on a circle or in a corner of the school, raised on the inside edge to a height of 18–24in. Approach in trot and ride away in canter, taking care not to override and key your horse up.

Suggested exercises: Labyrinth, Leg Circles, Neutral Pelvis, Pick Up Sticks, Promise Wrap, Raised Polework, Solo Polework, Tail Work, Walking the S, Wand Work, Wither Rocking, Zigzag

CATCHING, DIFFICULTY IN
See also Balance, lack of emotional, Bridle, difficult to, Headshy

Difficulty in catching a horse can be frustrating, but is not insoluble; you will need to adopt a long-term plan as well as a more immediate strategy.

Greed may get the better of some horses, so take some treats with you to tempt him with. Put them in your pocket or a bumbag ready to hand – don't take a bucket if there are other horses grazing because you could end up in the middle of a scuffle over it.

When grass is plentiful, your horse will be less reliant on you for food; treats will consequently be a less powerful attraction so you may need to restrict his grazing, either by turning him out in a smaller, barer paddock, or using electric fencing to reduce the area. He may also be more prepared to be caught if all his field companions are brought in first, leaving him on his own.

Leaving a headcollar on while he's turned out can make it easier to catch him, but use a 'breakaway' type which will give way if it gets caught on anything, and check his head daily for any signs of rubbing. Bear in mind it will also make it easier for thieves to catch him.

Do not try to corner him using a line of people or a long lunge rein to act as a moving barrier. Trapping him in this way can cause him to become frightened and defensive, and he may attempt to break through the human chain, lunge line or the fence in a blind panic. He may also try to kick out at anyone approaching him.

In the long term, you need to work out just why he doesn't want to be caught. Very often the only time we catch our horses is to do something for our own pleasure or convenience: even though he receives a feed each time he is brought in, for some horses the loss of liberty and being shut in a stable away from their field companions may seem a poor trade. He may associate being caught with always being ridden, so try to catch him up several times a day when you don't intend doing this, giving him a small food reward each time you are successful, and then letting him go again.

There are other ways you can make being caught a rewarding experience with pleasant

CATCHING TIPS

1. As you approach your horse, keep the headcollar and leadrope concealed behind your back, or looped over a shoulder so your hands look empty. Get as close as you feel you can, and then stand still; try to avoid staring him directly in the eye, which he may find intimidating or threatening.
2. Softly call his name, and slowly reach out a hand to offer a treat. Encourage him to come towards you to take it – if you step towards him, he'll probably move away if he is wary. Have several tempting treats ready in your pockets in case he's very cautious and you need to offer more than one.
3. Stand sideways on to him rather than facing him square on, so that as he becomes bolder and greedier for more treats and comes closer, he has to reach past in front of your body to reach them. This means that he'll end up almost beside you, instead of in front of you.
4. In this position, you can quietly slip the leadrope around his neck without alarming him into throwing his head up and backing away from you. Don't be tempted to hold him by just a handful of mane as this may cause him to pull away, and you won't be able to prevent him from breaking free.
5. Once you've captured him with the leadrope, praise him and give him another treat as a reward. Put the headcollar on whilst you are still standing beside him so you can do it without frightening him.

associations: spending a little time doing some Tellington TTouches (*see* Chapter 5) can make a massive difference to your relationship with each other and your horse's willingness to be caught.

Do not rule out pain as a possible cause of this problem. Feel the horse's neck for any signs of tension, and note how he responds to contact all over his body. Many horses that dislike being caught are tense and incorrectly muscled around the upper part of the neck. They may be ear shy, and dental problems (including dental changes in younger horses) can also create this problem, as the noseband of the headcollar may cause discomfort.

If your horse dislikes contact around the head and neck he is unlikely to let you put a headcollar on, and may gallop off the moment you release it. Horses that are sensitive to contact around the head can be tight in the tail, so working on the opposite end of your horse may also be beneficial. As well as giving a new and pleasant association with being caught,

Tellington TTouch body-work exercises will help to address any body tension that may be contributing to this problem.

If your horse struggles with the work you ask him to do or the way in which you ask him to do it, he will understandably be reluctant to let you catch him, so this is an aspect of your relationship which you should examine; similarly, if the environment he is brought into is stressful, or a place where he experiences abrupt or inconsiderate handling, he may not want to be caught.

Working on the ears may sound like a bizarre idea to help you catch your horse, but horses with this issue often have cold and/or tight ears and are frequently ear shy – and as explained in Part 2, by changing posture and releasing tension you can change his expectations and outlook on life, too. The exercise known as Ear Work (*see* below) can lower stress levels and also heart and respiratory rates; it encourages deep, rhythmical breathing, and promotes relaxation. It can also help high-headed horses learn to

EXERCISE: EAR WORK

1. Stand to the front and one side of your horse so you do not get hit in the face or stepped on if he suddenly throws his head up or moves forwards, and work on one ear at a time. If working on the left ear, stand on his left (near) side, resting the fingers of the left hand lightly on the headcollar noseband to support him while stroking the ear with your right hand and vice versa. Do not tie your horse up, or grip the headcollar tightly, or forcibly restrain your horse if he needs to move while doing this exercise.
2. Cup your hand around the base of the ear and gently but firmly stroke out along its length right to the tip, and then slide off the end. Repeat, moving the position of your hand slightly so that you cover every part of the ear.
3. Work slowly to calm and encourage relaxation; if using Ear Work to help combat the effects of shock, work more briskly and as you reach the ear tip where an acupressure shock point is located, add some circular movements with finger and thumb. Working the ear tip slowly can be beneficial for habitually nervous horses.

TOP LEFT: Stroke the ear from the base to the tip, changing your hand position slightly each time to ensure that you work the whole ear. This helps to release tension through the upper part of the neck and around the head, and can settle an anxious horse.

TOP RIGHT: Pay attention to the temperature at the tip of the ear. Many nervous horses and those that are ear shy have colder ear tips.

lower their heads and release through the poll, although they may be concerned initially about contact being made in this area. If your horse is very anxious, try stroking his ears flat against his head, if necessary using a soft sheepskin mitt on your hand, and wait until he is comfortable with you doing this before moving on to step 2.

Ear Work can also be life-saving, helping to prevent a horse from going into shock when in pain and waiting for veterinary attention – so if you only ever learn one Tellington TTouch, make it this one!

Suggested exercises: Clicker Targeting, Ear Work, Forelock Pulls, Mouth Work, Neck Work, Tail Work, Walking Up Behind

CHEWING
See also Girthing issues, Grooming issues, Pica, Stereotypies, Teeth, grinding

Not to be confused with crib-biting, some horses will chew on any wooden surfaces available – the tops of stable doors, kicking boards and partitions in the stable, wooden fencing and trees. This may have its roots in hunger due to insufficient forage in the stable or field, dietary deficiency, or boredom.

Youngsters will also often go through a less selective phase of chewing on anything and everything within reach – leadropes, buckets, saddlery, mucking out tools – even the handler's clothing can be targets. It may be linked to discomfort while teething, but mouthing objects is also very often simply part of the growing-up process, with the mouth being used to explore and gain more information about the environment. So don't leave things you value where they may get sampled; in the case of wooden field fencing, use electric fencing to create an inner barrier so it can't be reached; fence off or use cages to protect trees; and treat the tops of doors and surfaces in the stable with an unpleasant-tasting preparation. Prevention alone is not enough – you should also ensure regular turnout, provide sufficient forage and 'toys', and consult your vet if a deficiency is suspected. Remember that young horses as well as older ones need regular dental attention, and arrange for a visit from the vet/ equine dental technician.

A horse may bite at, or chew violently on his bridle reins or leadrope if discomfort is being caused by, for example, his being groomed or when the girth is being tightened. When riding, whilst it is quite acceptable for a horse to softly mouth the bit, if he is chewing excessively or grinding his teeth, this is also likely to be due to mouth discomfort or anxiety.

Suggested exercises: Belly Lifts, Body Wraps, Caterpillar, Ear Work, Jowl Release, Mouth Work, Tail Work

CLAUSTROPHOBIA
See also Bullying, Doors, Separation anxiety, Travelling

Some horses do appear to suffer from claustrophobia, although we don't really know whether it is the same as that experienced by people. Some horses may never have been stabled and be genuinely panicked by confinement, whilst others may have had a negative experience in the stable or trailer. They may have a poor association walking through narrow spaces such as doorways, or have problems walking under the door lintel and become extremely concerned going into or out of the stable as a result. Rushing through the doorway will increase the chances of injury, thus perpetuating their concerns.

It may also be caused by separation anxiety, and the problem may not be claustrophobia as such, but the fact of being taken away from a companion. Noise sensitivity can also be a factor as the horse may be worried by something he can hear but not see, and something as simple as moving the horse to a different stable may help him to overcome his fear. Whatever the cause, patience and training can go a long way to building his confidence, but care should be taken to ensure that he doesn't suffer a setback if he does seem to be improving.

Body-work and ground-work exercises that help the horse gain confidence and self-control, and which improve spatial awareness, will be extremely beneficial; the body work can be started outside on the yard or in an arena in the company of another horse if necessary. Once the horse is enjoying the body work (*see* Chapter 5) and is starting to relax, you can work on him in the stable if it is safe to do so. Many horses have been helped in this way,

EXERCISE: MOUTH WORK

Many horses are sensitive to contact in and around the mouth, so this is a great exercise with many practical applications. As well as helping with mouthing issues, it can help rebuild confidence regarding the head being touched and handled, and with bridling issues. It is also beneficial to use with horses which bite, are difficult to catch, are spooky, over-emotional, difficult to paste-worm, or which exhibit clingy behaviour.

1. Stand slightly to one side of the horse to enable easy access to the mouth area. Steady his head by holding the headcollar, and stroke down the nose and around the mouth and muzzle with the flat of your hand. If the horse is sensitive or defensive, use the back of your hand. If he dislikes being touched on one side, go back to the side that was more comfortable for him, then gradually work your way back round to the other side. Move the lips and chin in a circular motion with the palm of your hand, paying attention to your horse's body language at all times.
2. Once the horse is happy with you working around his mouth, lift his upper lip with your fingers or thumb, and keeping your fingers together, slide them back and forth over the top of the gum. If his mouth is dry, wet your hand first. If your horse bites, or has a strong upper lip, take great care and angle your hand so that the back of the hand is lifting the upper lip to ensure that your fingers remain safely away from his teeth.

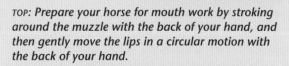

TOP: *Prepare your horse for mouth work by stroking around the muzzle with the back of your hand, and then gently move the lips in a circular motion with the back of your hand.*

LEFT: *If your horse is accepting contact around the outside of the mouth, gently lift the upper lip with your hand and, keeping your thumb and fingers well away from the teeth, rub your hand gently backwards and forwards along the upper gum at the front of the mouth. If your horse has a dry mouth then wet your hand first.*

3. When working the bottom gums, make small circles with your thumb on the inside of the lip, keeping your fingers outside on the horse's chin for support. Slide your thumb inside the corner of the mouth furthest away from you and make small circles on the inside of the cheek. Move the cheek gently away from the teeth while you do this to avoid being bitten. Check for any lacerations or soreness here that may indicate a dental problem. Then switch sides. If the horse moves his head round, go with the movement rather than restraining him. If he is really concerned, go back to doing TTouches somewhere else on the head or the body, or work the ears (see Ear Work in Catching, difficulty in).

Many horses that are tight in the mouth are also tight in the tail. If the horse cannot tolerate contact around the mouth, try starting with tail work (see Tail Work in Standing still), as this can be a useful stepping stone to helping the horse relax and release through his entire body.

Practise this exercise over several sessions if necessary, keeping them short – a little work goes a long way. If your horse knows that you will not force him to do anything he finds uncomfortable, trust between you will be established and he will be more willing to let you try again next time.

and enriching the stable environment with appropriate toys and positive experiences such as clicker training will also help him overcome his concerns. Build slowly over several days or weeks, and avoid the temptation to shut him in the stable too quickly.

Suggested exercises: Body Wraps, Clicker Targeting, Ear Work, Labyrinth, Mouth Work, Narrow Spaces Exercise, Walking over Plastic, Walking under Wands, Wand Work, ZigZag

CLIPPING
See also Grooming issues, Trimming up

Many horses are fearful of being clipped. Noise is often a major contributory factor, but there are many efficient rechargeable cordless machines, or ones that run off a portable battery pack, which are very much quieter than mains-operated clippers. The vibration – another source of concern – is also less, while a further advantage is that there is no trailing cord to scare the horse or pose a danger if it is trodden on. They also enable a clip to be completed more quickly than when constantly having to manoeuvre a long cable, and it is much easier to step safely away from a horse if it becomes fractious.

Competence as well as confidence in the operator are both important; it only takes one bad experience to make the horse apprehensive and less co-operative the next time. Blades must be sharp and the horse's coat clean and dry, otherwise they will tug painfully at the hairs. The environment can also make a difference. Some horses will be more relaxed outdoors than inside a stable where the potential for movement is more limited and the clippers may seem noisier – but wherever the job is done, ensure the footing is secure.

If the horse has a degree of concern about being clipped, there are several things you can do to develop his confidence, and that will help prepare a horse which has not been clipped before. For example, running the clippers near him will help accustom him to the noise; provide some hay for him to pick at to create pleasant associations. You can also ask someone else to hold the clippers while you do some

EXERCISE: JELLYFISH JIGGLES

As well as helping to accustom your horse to a vibrational feeling on his body as a preliminary step before using a massager or clippers, this is also a great exercise to use before riding as part of your warm-up routine. It will also help to prevent muscles from tightening after work.

1. Facing the side of your horse, place one hand lightly on his side and the other on the muscled part of his shoulder. Using the fingers and palm of one hand, make soft upward jiggling movements to the skin, creating an upward wave of movement.
2. Cover all the muscled area of the shoulder, neck, croup and hindquarters in this way, then repeat on the other side. When working on large areas of muscle such as on the quarters and croup, use both hands together, parallel to each other and with the thumbs nearly touching.

You can do this exercise with either one hand or two, depending on the sensitivity of your horse and the part of the body that you want to influence. Lay your hand gently on the horse's body, and vibrate the skin by jiggling your hand.

Tellington TTouches (*see* Chapter 5) to relax and settle him. Then gradually move the clippers closer to him until you can finally approach close enough to place one hand on his shoulder while holding the running clippers in the other. Be patient: it may take a while to reach this stage.

Stabling him where he can see another horse being clipped will be a further opportunity to familiarize him with the noise and to observe the procedure. You can also begin to accustom him to vibrating sensations by using a massager

– these can be bought quite cheaply – and Jellyfish Jiggle TTouches (*see* above).

Even with a normally quiet horse, never be complacent: when you are ready to start clipping, always start off at the shoulder area where he will be less anxious about what you are doing. If he is anxious or it is a new experience for him, only clip a small amount – just the underside of the neck and the front of the chest, or possibly even less, so he is not overwhelmed by the whole experience. As he becomes more confident you will be able gradually to progress to clipping larger areas. Leave the head until you have gained his trust, and if it really needs to be clipped, a bridle clip will look quite acceptable.

Some horses may be fine about being clipped in some places, but react defensively in others – most frequently when you are doing beneath the belly and between the thighs. Prepare him for being clipped in these areas by stroking along his belly and inside his thigh first with a wand, and then the flat of your hand. If he cannot tolerate this, he is unlikely to let you clip him here. If you do have to clip him before his sensitivity is reduced, wear a hard hat and have an assistant hold up a front leg on the same side as you to help inhibit a possible kick – but don't keep the leg up for long: if he panics when a leg is lifted you will need to work on his balance and confidence levels first. Keep your free hand in contact with his sides so you can feel any tension or contraction of the muscles which will give warning of a cowkick.

If your horse is fearful and you don't have your own clippers which you can use to spend time gradually accustoming him to, arrange for the vet to come and sedate him for the person doing the clipping. Do not use a twitch because it can make some horses worse, and can be painful, thereby adding to the horse's poor associations with clipping.

Be aware that the effects of sedation can wear off rapidly and sometimes with little warning, so be prepared not to be too fussy about what the finished clip looks like. A horse coming out of sedation and finding itself being clipped may react violently but without full motor control, and can therefore be dangerous.

Suggested exercises: Body Wraps (Full and Half wraps), Caterpillar, Jellyfish Jiggles, Lick of the Cow's Tongue, Tail Work, Wand Work

CLUMSINESS
See also Balance, Crookedness, Outline, Stiffness, Stumbling

Lack of co-ordination can be a youth thing, and growth spurts in youngsters can affect proprioceptive sense (the awareness of the postion of the body and limbs) in the same way as with children and teenagers. If a horse is croup high, either through conformation or during a growth spurt, his balance will be affected and his muscle memory may need to be changed – for example, he may have learnt to organize himself when walking downhill by swinging the hind limbs slightly out to the side. Poor foot and dental balance can also lead to issues with tripping, and of course any injury to, or restricted movement through, any of the joints or parts of the spine will also impede the horse's ability to move in balance.

Good rider posture and the appropriate fit of any equipment used on the horse are both of paramount importance when addressing any issue, since a narrow saddle or uneven rein contact will impinge on the horse's way of going and result in him 'leaving a leg behind' when working over poles. Lameness (which may be low grade and not always glaringly obvious), boredom and loss of concentration can be contributory factors too.

The neck is an important but often overlooked area. The horse primarily uses his neck to balance. It is made up of seven cervical vertebrae, the first two of which, the atlas and the axis, allow the head to nod up and down and to move from side to side. The other cervical vertebrae allow the neck to arch and bend.

Whilst breed type obviously determines the set and shape of the neck, tension or restricted movement in it will have a direct influence on stride length, body awareness, the ability to move forwards, proprioceptive sense, and the range of movement through the entire body, including the limbs and therefore collection.

Tension and poor muscle development in the upper part of the neck are usually evident in horses that struggle to work effortlessly in hand or under saddle.

Many problems in terms of both performance and behaviour can therefore be attributed to a poorly developed neck, and any tension present in it can inhibit proprioceptive sense, resulting in poor performance and clumsiness. If the neck is crooked, the rest of the body will compensate, and vice versa, so exercises aimed at improving the mobility and musculature of the neck, back and hindquarters can be key to helping a clumsy horse.

Your horse also relies upon his eyes (visual balance) and inner ear (vestibular balance) for stability and positional awareness. As both ears and eyes can be affected by tension in the upper part of the neck, muscle restriction around the upper cervical vertebrae will have a dramatic effect on the horse's ability to establish true self-carriage.

If a horse has poor core strength, tension through the limbs will be increased and movement restricted, so improving the overall posture of the horse so that he can use the correct muscles, ligaments and tendons for locomotion is important. You might also want to consider whether the clumsiness is due to fatigue or an incorrect diet, and it might be worth running some blood tests if this problem is ongoing.

Having investigated and either eliminated or remedied any physical issues, introducing polework exercises in hand and under saddle will increase motor skills and create greater self-awareness; they can also be good for increasing confidence and concentration as well as co-ordination and balance. Because they teach greater awareness and control of all four legs, and encourage an equal effort with them rather than favouring a dominant side, they also help to develop straighter movement and increased impulsion from behind.

As part of your preparation, practise good leading technique (*see* Leading issues); teach Wand Work, too, so you can use a wand to draw your horse's attention to his legs and feet or to help him slow or stop by touching him with it on the front of the chest or point of the shoulder furthest from you.

Making the transition from in-hand to ridden exercises will be easier if you first repeat the in-hand work with a saddle and tightened girth in place, as this will give the horse a different feel.

Although the work may appear simple to you, it requires high levels of physical co-ordination and intense concentration, which will be extremely tiring for the horse, so take care not to overdo things.

Suggested exercises: Balance Rein, Belly Lifts, Body Wrap, Caterpillar, Ear Work, Forelock Pulls, Jowl Release, Labyrinth, Leg Circles, Promise Wrap, Raised Poles, Shoulder Presses, Tail Work, Tracing the Arc, Wand Work, Wither Rocking, Work over Different Surfaces

---

EXERCISE: SOLO POLEWORK

Teach this exercise in hand first so your horse learns how to balance himself rather than relying on a rider for support; it also gives you the chance to observe him, which you can't do while mounted. Then try it while riding, when it will give both you as well as your horse new perceptions and further opportunities to refine balance and self-control.

1. Walk over the pole several times, noting what the horse does – does he speed up or slow down, move straight or crookedly, put in an extra half step or a longer unbalanced one, move his head up,

or touch it with any of his feet. This will give you a new insight into the horse's posture and movement, and a better understanding of why he may experience difficulties in certain areas.

2. Next, ask the horse to halt just in front of the pole – make sure you give him enough time to do so, as he may anticipate continuing.

3. Ask him to step forwards over the pole and halt again, this time standing with his front feet on one side and back feet on the other. Be patient, as he may find this difficult to manage at first.

4. Once the horse is comfortable stepping over and straddling the pole with front and back feet, you can start asking him to straddle it with his forelimbs; halt as before, but ask him to move just a single foot forward over it. He may not be able to maintain this for long: don't check him if he can't, but allow him to bring the other foot forward to join the first, pause for a moment, then praise him and walk on again. This can be especially difficult for a horse which is tight in the shoulder, high headed or on the forehand, but with each attempt he will learn how to reorganize posture and balance, becoming progressively more successful.

5. Most horses have a preference as to which foot is placed over the pole first. Notice which one the horse favours, and ask him to step over with the other instead. If he finds it a struggle, try stroking down the length of the leg with the wand to create awareness of it; if he's still a bit glued to the spot, tap gently on the front of the hoof wall with the hard button on the end of the wand handle to encourage him to lift that one over the pole first.

Once the horse is confident walking over a single pole, ask him to halt with his front legs over the pole. This may seem simple, but many horses that are nervous or disconnected through the hindquarters find this really difficult at first.

You can develop this exercise further by asking him to straddle the pole first with his front feet and then his hind feet. Horses that lack balance and those that are tight through the shoulders and back may struggle, but this is a brilliant exercise for improving co-ordination and gait.

6. Try changing the direction, leading from the other side, and moving the pole to a different place; you can also go on to develop the exercise further by asking him to straddle the pole with his back feet – though the front leg work must be properly established first, otherwise he will find it impossible. You can also teach him to move each forefoot in turn over the pole and then back again.

This work can be invaluable in teaching him how to adjust his weight distribution so that he finds balancing whilst travelling easier; also, being able to ask him to step forwards one foot at a time on cue can be helpful when loading.

EXERCISE: LICK OF THE COW'S TONGUE

Try this TTEAM exercise which raises the back and helps soften stiff, tight back muscles before putting the saddle on. It will also enhance suppleness and co-ordination, and will soothe sore, overworked muscles after a demanding work session or competition.

1. Stand by the side of your horse, next to the girth area and facing towards him. Stroke gently but firmly – don't tickle – with the flat of your hand along his belly.

2. If he is relaxed about that, place one hand lightly on his body and the palm of the other, fingers pointing away from you, under his belly just past the midline. Keep the fingers slightly apart and gently curved. Start on or just behind the girth area.

TOP: *Place the flat of your hand on or near the girth area near the middle line.*

BOTTOM: *Gently slide your hand up in a straight line over the ribs.*

3. Draw your hand up and around the ribcage in a long, continuous sweeping stroke. As your hand moves up the side of the ribcage, rotate it so the fingers point towards the spine, and continue the upward sweep, up to and just over the spine.
4. Repeat the movement, moving your hand one hand's breadth across from where you made the first, and continue in this way until you have covered the whole of the belly area. If your horse is ticklish, just work on those areas where he is comfortable.

Turn your hand around so that your wrist is not bent, and continue sliding your hand up over the rib cage towards the spine.

Finish the movement by lifting your hand just before you reach the spine, but ensure that you slide over the back. Repeat the movement along the horse's body, but if at any point your horse lifts a leg, tries to bite, pins his ears back or moves away, go back to where contact was acceptable.

COLD BACKED

See also Bucking, Girthing issues, Saddling issues, Spooking

An increasingly common problem for many horses, cold-backed behaviour may range from hunching or dipping the back when the saddle is placed on it or as the girth is tightened, to actually collapsing to the ground. The horse may be reluctant to walk forwards when the rider is on board, he may 'freeze' (*see* Chapter 1) when girthed and/or mounted, or demonstrate more explosive behaviour such as bucking and plunging.

There can be a variety of contributory factors for this behaviour, and a thorough veterinary examination to rule out the possibility of, for example, kissing spines or soft tissue damage should be your first concern. It may also be linked to the sensation of the girth being tightened causing a sudden drop in blood pressure – and of course, poor saddle fit is another possible cause.

Sensitivity and/or blocked awareness through the back, tension through the loins and around the girth area, a tight or floppy tail, and a cold area on each side of the withers, are symptoms often found in horses that suffer from this syndrome, and exercises aimed at improving movement and circulation through the neck and back, and reducing tension around the girth area, will be of benefit.

The horse may also panic, go into freeze, or become defensive in his behaviour when you enter the stable with the saddle, and it is important to pay attention to the body language of the horse so that you can address his concerns before his behaviour escalates.

You will need to break down the saddling and girthing process into individual stages; stroking down the chest and front legs with a wand, Ear Work, and the exercises for lowering his head and neck to keep him relaxed and above all breathing, will all be beneficial both before and while you slowly tack him up. Working him in hand with a half wrap can be another useful step.

Suggested exercises: Belly Lifts, Ear Work, Half Wrap, Labyrinth, Lick of the Cow's Tongue, Stroking the Line, Tail Work, Walking the S, Wand Work

COPROPHAGIA

See also Pica, Stereotypies

Young foals will often eat small amounts of their mother's droppings as a way of helping to establish the gut microflora essential to digestion, and of providing additional minerals and vitamins; this practice may also help in building up immunity, protecting the gut from viral and bacterial infections, and is thought to play a part in learning about food selection.

While a normal behaviour in youngsters, by five or six months it should have disappeared; if it persists or is observed in adult horses it may be due to insufficient fibre or protein in the diet, lack of certain vitamins, minerals and/or trace elements, or if stabled, the behaviour may arise as a result of boredom. It may also temporarily occur if the horse has received antibiotic treatment which can disrupt gut microflora; using probiotics will be a better way of restoring efficient gut function.

Otherwise, increasing exercise, turn-out and forage may be the answer, but a vet and equine nutritionist should be consulted. Supplementation may be suggested, but should be used under professional guidance, as excesses can create further dietary imbalances, and can be harmful.

Suggested exercises: Belly Lifts, Ear Work, Mouth Work

COWS, FEAR OF

See Other Animals, Fear of

COWKICKING

See also Aggression, Clipping, Grooming issues, Laziness, Nappiness

Kicking forwards beneath the belly with a hind leg is usually a response to discomfort, such as colic, rough grooming round the more sensitive and ticklish areas beneath the belly, flanks and between the thighs, or the girth pinching or being tightened too abruptly. It may also happen when the horse is being ridden if the rider uses over-strong, punishing leg aids to ask the horse to go forwards.

Sometimes it may be impossible to avoid causing a degree of either discomfort or concern – as when cleaning and treating an injury, for example. Wear a hard hat, and ask someone to hold up a foreleg; while this won't entirely prevent a cowkick it will reduce its scope, range and power. Do not keep the foreleg up for long. If your horse is worried about having a leg held, draw the tail to the side that you are working on so that the horse's weight is on the hind leg nearer to you, thereby minimizing the chances of being cowkicked.

Suggested exercises: Belly Lifts, Ear Work, Forelock Pulls, Tail Work, Wand Work

CRIB BITING

See Stereotypies

CROOKEDNESS

See also Canter, favouring a lead, Outline, Stiffness

All horses are one-sided to some degree, causing crookedness in movement. This may be due to natural asymmetry, uneven musculature from incorrect schooling, physical trauma, rider crookedness and/or excessive emphasis of the aids on one side.

Crookedness will be accentuated if free forward movement is suppressed by over-containment with the hands, so may be especially apparent in an over-fresh, under-exercised horse. It sometimes occurs when riding downhill, when it may be due to poor balance, but can also indicate poor saddle fit when the gradient causes increased pressure from the points of the saddle tree to be placed on the muscles behind the shoulders.

On the weak/hollow side, because the inside hind leg tends to step to the side rather than directly forwards beneath the horse's body, an unequal length of stride between the left and right hind is produced, which can make the horse look unlevel. It will also limit forward impulsion and the ability to lengthen stride.

Minimize the tendency to crookedness when schooling by repeating the work done on one rein on the other, and do not ask for more bend on the weak/hollow side than you can obtain on the more difficult, stiffer side. Pay attention to trotting diagonals, while accurately ridden school figures such as circles, turns and serpentines, as well as work in straight lines and lateral work, will be beneficial in increasing lateral suppleness and straightness.

Rider straightness will obviously be a major influence on the horse's movement, and a crooked rider will never be able to straighten a crooked horse. However, it can be hard for the rider to maintain straightness, especially as the senses can be deceptive, so do seek help from someone on the ground. This is where ground work can be particularly helpful, in that you can do a lot to help improve the situation without the need to be actually on the horse's back, so you won't inadvertently be reinforcing habitual incorrect postures.

Suggested exercises: Caterpillar, Clicker Targeting, Labyrinth, Leg Circles, Neutral Pelvis, Solo Polework, Tracing the Arc, Walking the S, Wither Rocking

EXERCISE: TRACING THE ARC

This is a Connected Riding exercise which can highlight and help resolve any imbalance between the left and right rein. It helps to reduce tension in the poll, temporal mandibular joint (TMJ) and neck, and will also help the horse to develop straightness and an even rein contact.

Although a seemingly simple exercise, it can be quite difficult for some horses, and those which have worked consistently on the forehand with a significant amount of tension through the neck may find it hard initially. The handler can help prepare the horse for this exercise by using Mouth Work to help him focus, and Forelock Circles and Slides (see Key to Exercises).

If the horse cannot tolerate you standing in front of him, or finds it hard to stand still, work on other exercises first.

1. The noseband of the headcollar or bridle needs to be relatively snug for this exercise. Stand in front of your horse with your thumb and index fingers hooked near the middle of the noseband, supporting it lightly with both hands. The horse's neck should be as straight as possible. Imagine a horizontal arc that begins and ends in line with the shoulders of the horse. You are standing at the top or middle of the arc.

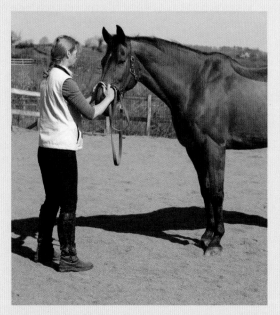 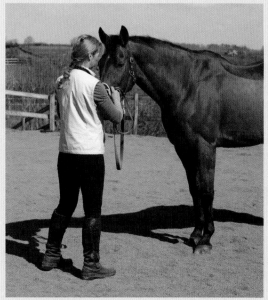

LEFT: *Stand in front of the horse and rest your fingers on the noseband. Avoid gripping the noseband in case the horse lifts his head. Wait for a moment until the horse is relaxed. If he panics or braces against the contact, try some of the other exercises aimed at releasing tension in the neck first.*

RIGHT: *Imagine there is an arc in front of your horse and that you are standing at the top of that arc. Take one small step to the right and see if the horse can move his neck as you move. His front feet should remain in the same position. If he throws up his head or moves his legs he is tight in the neck. Do not force him to bend. The aim is to help your horse soften and release. If he can flex gently take another step to the right and then move back to the starting point one step at a time. Repeat the exercise in the opposite direction. Pause after each step so that your horse processes the information and has time to release before you ask him to flex again.*

Soften through your knees, hips and back and keep the arms light – if you lean on the headcollar you will encourage your horse to brace through his neck to compensate for your lack of balance.

2. Take one small step to the left. Pause to allow the horse to release his head and poll. Slowly take one or two more small steps to the left, pausing to allow for the release each time, and with your feet following the line of the imaginary arc. Then take small steps to the right, still pausing and allowing for the release after each step until you are back where you started. Repeat the exercise, stepping to the right each time.

3. You are aiming for fluidity of movement, although at the beginning you may feel that your horse gets 'stuck' or that the movement is jerky – remember to keep your steps tiny and check that you aren't bracing in your own posture and creating tension in your hand. Note whether your horse finds it easier to move in one direction than the other; this will correspond to the way he moves under saddle. You may only be able to achieve a few steps in both directions at first, but as your horse begins to release through the poll and through the neck you should be able to increase the range of movement by moving further along the curve of the imaginary arc.

CROWDING
See Leading

DISMOUNTING, DIFFICULTIES IN
See also Balance, Halting, Mounting, Standing still

Difficulties when dismounting are often due to similar issues as when mounting. Check the saddle fit carefully, as extra pressure tends to be placed on the front arch of the saddle, so any tightness in fit or soreness in the shoulder may result in the horse reacting. The sudden movement of the rider can also be alarming for some horses, so although you should try to dismount athletically, try also to do so without excessively exaggerating your movement.

Suggested exercises: Crest Release, Sliding Numnahs, Walking over Plastic, Walking under Wands, ZigZag

DISUNITED CANTER
See Canter, disunited

DOGS, FEAR OF
See Other animals, fear of

DONKEYS, FEAR OF
See Other animals, fear of

DOOR, CLIMBING OVER
See also Bullying, Claustrophobia, Separation anxiety

A horse that for some reason cannot cope with confinement in the stable may try to escape, either by pushing through the door as someone opens it, or if it is shut, by jumping or climbing out over it. Closing the top door or fitting a metal grid will further isolate the horse from the outside world and may cause his stress levels to escalate even more: neither of these options deals with the underlying cause, and as the horse becomes increasingly distressed he may throw himself around in the stable, kick out at the walls, and become dangerous to approach.

To resolve the problem you will first need to identify the cause: it may be a case of simply changing to a different stable, or the issues may be more complex and take more time to work through, including separation anxiety, claustrophobia, lack of experience of being in a stable, or perhaps in the past

EXERCISE: SLIDING NUMNAHS

As well as increasing confidence about passing through narrow openings, this is a great exercise to help reduce concern in horses that are nervous about rider movement. It's a good preliminary to wearing rugs and a saddle for youngsters, as well as a preparation for being backed – and if you ever fall off your horse, it will teach him to stop and wait for you instead of running off.

1. Ask someone to hold the horse while you very gently put on a numnah or saddle cloth. If he is a little concerned about it, or if this is the first time he's had anything placed on his back, use a very small pad at first or even a folded stable rubber, progressing to a larger numnah as his confidence develops. Let him check it out first if he wants; putting a little food on it will help create a positive association. You and your assistant should stay on the same side in case the horse steps sideways away from the movement of the numnah.

Place a numnah on the horse and ask your helper to walk him forwards for a few paces. Gently pull the numnah off the horse as he walks, and use your voice to give him the cue to stop by saying 'Aaaaaand whoooooooaaaa'. Ask your helper to back up your verbal cue if necessary. Gently place the numnah on the floor and put some small treats on it. Watch for signs that your horse may be concerned. Lip licking can be a sign of stress and is not always a signal that the horse is starting to relax.

2. Practise sliding the numnah off, keeping hold of it and offering a few treats from on top of it. Once the horse is relaxed about this, draw the numnah off to the side and let it drop gently to the ground. Quickly place a little food on it – if he doesn't realize it's there, gently guide his head round to it.

3. When he's quite settled about this, ask your assistant to lead him forwards while you walk beside him, holding the numnah in place with one hand. Once again slowly slide the numnah off and place some food on top. The moment the numnah begins to move, your assistant should ask the horse to halt – make sure you communicate clearly with her so she knows when to cue him to stop.

4. Most horses learn this exercise very quickly and have very positive associations with the numnah. Practise it from both sides, as some horses may be fine on one side, but a little apprehensive about the other. Once the horse starts to halt as he feels the numnah sliding off without needing to be cued by your assistant you can introduce variable reinforcement – where he doesn't receive a food

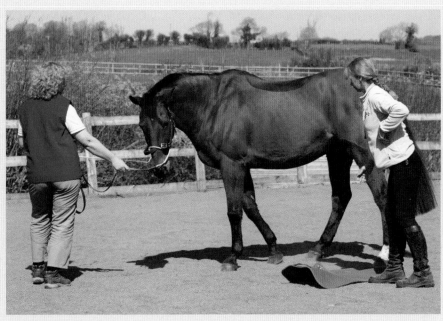

Most horses will turn to look, but if he is worried, encourage him to look at the cloth on the floor and make sure that he sees you putting some treats on it.

Avoid letting him grab the cloth with his teeth in a bid to snatch the food. Most horses learn in one session that the sensation of something slipping from their back is a signal to stop and that contact on the body from an object is nothing to fear. This helps them to be more thoughtful and move beyond their instinctive responses.

reward every time, but unpredictably every second, third or fourth repetition instead – as otherwise some individuals may become irritable if an anticipated treat isn't forthcoming. This will also encourage him to think about what he's doing instead of only focusing on the food aspect of the exercise.

he has been frightened when stabled. Until the horse's confidence in being in the stable is restored, it will be unfair and potentially dangerous to keep him in, and he will have to live out; however, feeding him in an open-sided field shelter which he can enter or leave as he wishes can be a good way of getting him used to the idea.

Suggested exercises: Body Wraps, Ear Work, Wand Work

DOOR, KICKING AT
See also Pawing, Separation anxiety

This is a common behaviour in many horses at feed times, or if stable companions go out to the field or for a ride, leaving him behind, and is most frequently due to frustration and/or impatience. The noise can be irritating and damaging to the door, but more seriously this habit can be injurious to your horse's legs.

Make sure your horse has sufficient forage; giving him a portion of his ration to nibble at before his concentrate feed is due will take the edge off his appetite and keep him occupied. Shutting the top door temporarily while feeds are given out may stop him striking out with a front foot, but may cause him to kick out with one or both back feet at the stable walls instead, which can lead to back and hock injuries and may frighten neighbouring horses. Padding the inside of the stable door with heavy rubber matting will protect his legs and the door to a certain extent; in warm weather, fitting a breast bar or webbing gate and leaving the lower door open removes a barrier for him to kick at altogether, although he may then paw at the ground instead. You could also teach him to move away from his door at feed times by using clicker target training.

Suggested exercise: Clicker Targeting

DOOR, OPENING
See also Chewing

Mouthing at and playing with the top bolt of the stable door can lead to your horse accidentally sliding it across and opening it – and he may then learn to do this intentionally. It is not unknown for such escape artists to then not only let themselves out, but to go around the yard letting others out, too! Prevention is the only solution, so fit an enclosed 'horse-proof' bolt. Don't economize by using a trigger or spring clip from a leadrope, as the horse will still fiddle with it, and many nasty injuries to lips which have been caught in them have occurred as a result of this practice. Never padlock the top bolt in case it is necessary to release the horse quickly in an emergency.

This is often a behaviour adopted by horses which are bored and do not have enough to occupy them, so ensure they have sufficient exercise and turn-out time, and when they are stabled, provide them with sufficient forage to pick at, and stable toys for their additional entertainment.

DOOR, REFUSAL TO GO THROUGH
See also Bullying, Claustrophobia, Door, climbing over, Door, rushing through, Travelling

This behaviour is usually due to concern about what lies ahead, perhaps because the horse is being asked to enter an enclosed space, cannot see what is inside, is intimidated by a neighbouring horse, or associates it with a previously alarming or painful experience such as the door blowing shut against his hips, or banging his head on a low lintel. Don't try to force him forwards, as this is likely to confirm any fears; turn on any lights and allow time for his eyes to adjust; and open doors wide and secure them back in windy weather. Offering food, and stroking the leadrope (or bridle reins if leading in a bridle) can help encourage him forwards, whilst also encouraging a lowered head carriage; and teaching him confidence-building exercises may help him cope with any concerns he has about moving through narrow spaces.

Suggested exercises: Clicker Targeting, Dingo, Narrow Spaces Exercise, Sliding Numnahs, Solo Polework, Stroking the Line, Walking under Wands, Wand Work

DOOR, RUSHING THROUGH
See also Bullying, Claustrophobia, Gateways

A horse that rushes through a door or gateway often does so because he is anxious – most frequently because he has banged a hip on the doorframe, or the door has blown shut on him before he was fully through. Some horses have poor proprioceptive sense and spatial awareness, which may add to their concerns, and the more a horse rushes the worse this may become, increasing the likelihood of him catching himself and further reinforcing his fears. Increasing his sense of self-awareness and improving his balance, and teaching him to move one step at a time, as well as the Narrow Spaces Exercise (*see* problem 'Gateways, reluctant to go through'), will all be of benefit.

Other suggested exercises: Body Wrap, Clicker Targeting, Labyrinth, Narrow Spaces Exercise, Promise Wrap, Sliding Numnahs, Solo Polework, Wand Work

DRINK, REFUSAL TO
See also Bullying

When away from home some horses may be suspicious of, and reluctant to drink, water from a different source, and there may be a risk of dehydration as a result. Adding apple juice can help disguise the smell and taste, although it is advisable to accustom the horse to this at home, otherwise it may still be viewed with suspicion. When competing away from

home, offer your horse a well soaked haynet to nibble at on the journey, and if you think he may refuse to drink the water available at the showground, take a supply of your own water with you too.

If the problem is occurring at home, it may be that your horse is being bullied out in the field or in a neighbouring stable, and is fearful of approaching the water supply in the field. Dehydration can be as much of a problem in winter as summer, as horses will drink less if the water is very cold, so take the chill off by adding warm water to his water bucket in the stable. Make sure ice is cracked on water troughs during freezing weather.

Horses may also be quite fastidious about the cleanliness of water and containers, so clean out and refill buckets daily and field troughs on a weekly basis. Make sure you also provide some kind of ramp or escape route from troughs for wildlife. Ammonia from wet bedding or under rubber matting may also be a contributory factor, so ensure that the horse's stable smells fresh and clean.

If your horse appears to be drinking more water than usual, with no obvious reason for it such as warmer weather, increased exercise or dry forage intake, consult your vet as it may indicate a health problem. Make sure that he is able to drink when out in the field as some horses will guard the water supply and not just food.

Suggested exercises: Ear Work, Mouth Work

DROPPINGS, EATING
See Coprophagia

EATING, CHANGES IN
See also Bedding, eating, Bullying, Coprophagia, Pica

Not all horses are greedy – some can be quite finicky, often those which are more nervous/anxious in temperament. It may help to look at ways in which their environment, management and work can be made less stressful, plus the use of Tellington TTouches (*see* Chapter 5) to further relax such horses and further reduce their stress levels. Probiotics can be a useful addition to their feed, as disturbance to the gut flora can be a contributory factor.

If the horse usually eats up, refusal of food may be due to contamination, change of feed stuff, mustiness due to poor storage or keeping beyond the 'use by' date, or to dirty feed buckets with soured, encrusted deposits. Adding honey, apple juice or molasses to the food may help to disguise the presence of supplements or medications, although more suspicious horses may still refuse to eat if they are unfamiliar with these scents and tastes. If it is essential for the horse to take such additives or medicines, another method of administration may be advisable.

Sometimes horses on a high concentrate ration will go off their feed for no apparent reason. Reduce the amount offered and increase the forage ration, and investigate alternative ways of providing energy in a more concentrated form. Most feed manufacturers provide helplines so you can consult an equine nutritionist for advice on creating an appropriately balanced diet.

Horses are by nature selective grazers and like variety as well as choice, so adding succulents such as sliced apples, carrots, parsnip, swedes, turnips and sugar beet, or using beet water, apple juice, diluted honey or treacle to dampen feeds, will help both to fulfil this aspect and tempt shy feeders.

Changes in eating habits may also indicate a health problem, whether it is an increase in or loss of appetite; keep a close eye on your horse, rather than dismissing it as either greed or fussiness, and consult your vet. Where a horse is abnormally slow in eating, dental or other mouth problems may be responsible (*see* Chapter 3) and should be investigated and dealt with as a matter of some urgency. In the meantime offer softer foods that need less chewing, soften hay by soaking or steaming, and if necessary supplement forage with chaff.

If the horse is stabled next to another that he finds intimidating and can see through an adjoining partition, he may be reluctant to approach his feed and eat. Anxiety caused by the close proximity of another horse can also be the cause of bolting food; this may also extend to humans, so don't groom or muck out while he is eating, but allow him some peace and quiet. Eating fast can lead to choking as well as to poorly chewed food, which will therefore be less efficiently digested, so is to be discouraged as far as is possible. Hunger may be responsible: ensure he has sufficient bulk in the form of forage and give a portion of it before offering the concentrate ration to take the edge off his appetite. Try to keep feed times as regular as possible, too, since if your horse is fretting over when his meals are going to arrive, he may become even more likely to bolt it.

Adding chaff to the concentrate ration will slow eating and encourage better chewing, but avoid adding lumps of food such as carrots and apples if the horse is inclined to bolt his food because of the risk of choking: if you want to add such succulents, grate rather than slice them into the feed, which should also be well dampened. Placing a large lump of rock salt in the feed bowl may help to slow some horses down, but others may simply become frustrated and will strike out with a forefoot, paw at the ground or tip the bowl over.

Feeding from the floor is better for both digestion and dentition, but if in his impatience while eating the horse kicks at his bucket and tips it over, try placing it within a suitably sized car tyre. If there is room to do so, do away with a feed bowl altogether and clear a space on the floor where you can scatter the food along so he cannot gulp down large mouthfuls. Food-dispensing toys can be another way of slowing down the eating process, and can help to alleviate boredom for a stabled horse.

Suggested exercises: Belly Lifts, Caterpillar, Ear Work, Forelock Slides and Circles, Mouth Work, Rotating the Pelvis

ESCAPING, FROM FIELD
See also Door, climbing over, Separation anxiety

Escaping may be by accident, for example where weak areas of fencing give way or a battery powering electric fencing runs down. Some horses do learn to open gate catches, especially if these are weak and easy to move, but it is usually easy to foil them by placing a chain round the gate and gatepost on the latch side. Where a horse is a habitual as opposed to an accidental escapee, increasing the height of the fence will not always deter him and he may still attempt to jump it. Using electric fencing to create an inner barrier may be more effective as it will make the boundary wider and more imposing, and will also discourage him from leaning on it to break it down. Any electric fencing used should always be highly visible. Adding a lower rail to fencing or a second, lower line of electric fencing will prevent him from rolling beneath it.

Improving field security may solve the problem, but you should also try to determine the reason for your horse wanting to escape, otherwise he may continue to try to do so and injure himself in the attempt. If he is being bullied, find company for him which he finds more amenable; or maybe he is on his own and wants some company.

Lack of keep in the field may also lead to breakouts, in which case provide forage. If the horse is being kept on poor grazing intentionally because of weight issues, provide low calorie bulk in the form of soaked hay, and enrich his environment by providing large roots such as swedes as edible toys – you can also scatter strips of carrot, apples and other succulents around the area for him to 'discover' and browse on.

Many horses are stabled from the moment they are started and some will not have had access to pasture for many, many years. Just as some horses suffer from claustrophobia, some seem to experience agoraphobia, so in such a case build up the horse's confidence by turning him out for short periods in an enriched paddock, and gradually extend the length of turn-out over time.

ESCAPING, FROM STABLE
See also Claustrophobia, Door, climbing over, Door, opening, Door, rushing through

Some horses learn to let themselves out accidentally through playing with the door bolt, but others learn to intentionally push past a person opening the door and escape. You can stop this behaviour by teaching your horse to move back from door when you want to enter by using clicker target training, but while working on this, fitting a breastbar or webbing door-gate across the interior of the doorway will make it possible for you to enter by ducking underneath without the horse attempting to barge out past you each time.

Suggested exercise: Clicker Targeting

FEED, BOLTING
See Eating

FEET, DIFFICULT TO PICK UP
See also Balance, Feet, difficult to shoe, Standing still

Ideally, horses should be taught to have their legs handled and feet picked up from a young age, but not all are so fortunate in either good or adequate handling. If a horse is lacking in confidence or anxious about having his legs touched, use a wand to initially make contact in a way that is safe for you and which avoids being confrontational or forceful with him.

EXERCISE: WITHER ROCKING

This exercise can help release tight shoulders and withers, and is helpful in teaching the horse to transfer his weight from one side to the other. Performing it will enable you to see the habitual pattern of bracing that most horses have, and you may find that the horse struggles to transfer his weight on to one particular foreleg. The most common pattern that horses develop is to load the near fore, and this exercise can help to address this problem and to encourage him to weight his limbs more evenly – this in turn will make it easier for him to balance and to stand still.

This exercise will also lengthen the stride, and encourage lift through the back and improved hind-limb engagement; it can also be used to help create controlled forward movement in a horse that has become 'stuck' or gone into 'freeze' (see Chapter 1).

1. This exercise can be done while the horse is standing still, or in hand while he is moving. Place one hand palm down over the withers, cupping the highest point.
2. Place one foot in front of the other and keep your hips and knees slightly flexed and soft. Keeping an even connection through your arm and hand, slowly transfer your weight forwards on to your front foot. This will send the withers away from you.
3. Pause for a moment, and then slowly transfer your weight on to your back foot. This will bring the withers towards you. Repeat this a few times. Note whether one side is freer than the other, and pay attention to how the horse reorganizes himself during this exercise. If he is tight through the shoulders, has sensitive withers, or has spent a significant amount of time loading one limb unevenly, he may struggle with this exercise, as any change in habitual posture can make a horse feel unsafe.
4. If the horse is really braced through the withers or is sensitive to contact on the top of them, try placing the flat of your right hand on the shoulder and make a small suggestion with your hand that the horse move slightly away from you. Hold this position if the horse is comfortable, and then slowly allow the shoulder to move back towards you as you maintain a supportive contact.

Hold the line in the outside hand if you are working the horse in hand, and place your other hand gently on the horse's body. Stand with your feet apart and rock on to the outside leg, which will bring the horse's body towards you. Transfer your weight on to the other leg, taking the withers away from you. You may note that the horse can move easily in one direction but not the other. Keep the movement slow and fluid and note whether the horse moves off, moves away or braces himself against you. This exercise helps him transfer his weight from one foot to another, and will help you to recognize any balance issues that the horse may have.

Many difficulties encountered when picking up feet are caused through lack of consideration by the handler: lifting the foot up too high – which often happens with adults picking out ponies' feet – or drawing it out to the side, which can be uncomfortable for the horse and may cause him to lose his balance so he is forced to stamp his foot back down. Young horses will find it hard to stand on three legs for very long, while older or arthritic horses may find it painful to flex their joints; lameness and back problems may also be a source of discomfort when feet are picked up, so ask your vet to examine your horse if he seems to be struggling, and if necessary refer you to an equine physiotherapist.

When picking up a horse's feet, rather than tying him up, which will restrict movement, ask someone to hold him so he can move his head and neck freely, and easily adjust his balance through his whole body. Make sure the ground is level, and that the horse is standing in a balanced way.

Ask him to pick a foot up by sliding your hand down his leg to just above the fetlock joint, and then gently but firmly pinch with the forefinger and thumb between the base of the cannon bone and tendon. If he is 'stuck', go to another leg and repeat the exercise and experiment by giving an ask-and-release signal with your thumb and fingers on a different part of the tendon. When he lifts the foot let him put it back down and then go back to the more difficult side. Some horses do find it very difficult to transfer their weight from the feet on one side to the other and can become very planted – teaching the wither-rocking exercise (*see* opposite) can help solve this problem.

Having lifted the foot, keep it beneath the horse's shoulder/quarters, and when putting it down again, place it on the floor – don't just drop it, as this can unbalance the horse, and also creates an uncomfortable ricochet effect which travels up the leg through the joints. If he

panics, try gently rocking the fetlock so that the lower leg moves slightly up and down. Go with the movement if he wriggles, and avoid holding on too persistently as this will frighten him. Remember that standing on three legs isn't natural for horses – some have trouble standing still on all four legs, never mind three – so this is an action which needs to be taught, and it will take time for the horse to learn how to do it comfortably and in balance. It can also be tiring, so don't ask the horse to hold up a foot for too long.

Suggested exercises: Balance Rein, Leg Circles, Raised Poles, Solo Polework, Sternum Lifts, Tail Work, Wand Work, Wither Rocking

FEET, DIFFICULT TO SHOE
See also Balance, Feet, difficult to pick up, Standing still

If your horse finds it difficult to balance standing on three feet, it is likely that he will struggle to cope when the farrier visits to trim and shoe him, so for the safety of all and to ensure that unpleasant associations aren't formed, spend some time teaching him this necessary skill.

As the farrier will need to move each foot out to the side in order to carry out trimming and shoeing, once you have taught your horse to pick up his feet, begin to teach the required balance, and increase the range of movement through the shoulder and hip joints, by doing the exercise Leg Circles (*see* below). Doing this just before a visit from the farrier will also help experienced horses to feel more comfortable. If you know that your horse suffers from balance or stiffness issues, do inform your farrier before he starts work so that he can take care not to lift the feet too high.

If you have a youngster which has not been shod before, stabling him nearby while other horses are being shod will help accustom him to the noise and smell. If your horse is young

EXERCISE: LEG CIRCLES

This exercise increases the flexibility of the limbs and the shoulder and neck muscles, improves balance, and eases tension in the back. Performed before exercise, you will notice improved freedom of movement in all four limbs.

1. Stand next to your horse, facing towards his quarters. Stroke down the back of the foreleg next to you until you reach the fetlock, and ask him to pick up his foot.
2. As his foot comes up, support the fetlock joint with the hand closest to the horse, and cradle his hoof with the other one. Keep your thumb over the shoe and your fingers cupping the front of the hoof, and avoid flexing the fetlock joint. Keeping your knee and hip joints flexed, rest your outside elbow on your outside knee or thigh for support to protect your back from injury.
3. Gently circle the hoof just above the spot on the ground where it was resting. Allow the movement to be created by moving your body rather than just your hands. Circle the hoof the same number of times in both clockwise and anti-clockwise directions.
4. Do not lift the hoof higher or make the circles bigger than your horse is comfortable with, and do not pull the leg out to the side. Circle the hoof at gradually decreasing distances from the ground, until finally the toe is resting on it. If he is very stiff or unbalanced he may not be able to rest his toe on the ground, in which case just get as close to it as you can.
5. Repeat with the other foreleg, and then with each of the hind legs. When lifting a back foot, support the cannon bone with your inside hand.

FAR LEFT: *Support the front hoof with your outside hand and keep your thumb on the bottom of the hoof to prevent the horse lifting his foot and catching you in the face. Support the fetlock joint with the other hand, and avoid flexing the fetlock. Rest your outside arm on your outside thigh and move your body in a circular movement which will naturally circle the horse's leg. Ensure that you do not pull the leg out to the side.*

LEFT: *Repeat the exercise with the hind leg, but this time support the hind cannon bone instead of the fetlock.*

EXERCISE – NARROW SPACES EXERCISE

Set up this exercise to help develop confidence about going through narrow spaces such as doorways and gateways; it can also be invaluable for helping with trailer and lorry loading issues.

1. Make a barrier using stacked bales of bedding, or a jump pole suspended between jump wings with rugs or blankets hung over it to make it look more solid.
2. Lead the horse past this barrier, keeping yourself between it and him in case he moves sideways away from it. Position yourself level with his head rather than his shoulder (see Leading issues) as you will have more control in this position, and keep to the side so you don't get knocked over if he begins to hurry forwards. Stay at a distance he feels safe, and allow him to look at and investigate it if he wishes. Halt each time just before it, again as you are level with it, and once more just after passing it, so he learns to steady and think about what he is doing rather than panicking and rushing. If you have introduced clicker training, you can use a clicker to help mark calm behaviour which you want him to repeat.
3. As his confidence grows, gradually begin passing closer by the barrier; when he is settled about this, introduce a second parallel barrier. Make the distance fairly wide between them, and repeat the exercise, halting just before, in the middle and on reaching the end of the tunnel. If the horse finds it difficult to halt in the middle or begins to rush, increase the distance between the two barriers.
4. As the horse becomes more assured, gradually begin to decrease the distance between the barriers. When he is confidently performing the exercise you can also try riding through it, introducing it under saddle following the same steps as in hand.

Build on this exercise so that the horse is walking between two 'barriers', and gradually decrease the distance between the obstacles, over several sessions if necessary. At each stage make sure that the horse can stop in between and after the obstacles, and be sure to let him look around. If you restrict the movement in his head and neck the horse is more likely to panic and swing his body around, which may cause him to hit the barriers and will reinforce his concerns.

and/or anxious, discuss it with the farrier and consider spreading out the work on his feet over several short sessions rather than doing everything in one go, which may be too much for him to deal with both physically and mentally.

Hold your horse while he is being shod, rather than tying him up, so he can see what is going on, and reassure him if necessary. Choose a level area for him to stand on, and use a fly spray in the summer so he isn't bothered by insects which may make him fidget. In cold weather try to find somewhere sheltered, out of the way of cold breezes, and rug him up to keep him warm.

Suggested exercises: Balance Rein, Leg Circles, Solo Polework, Sternum Lifts, Tail Work, Wand Work, Wither Rocking

GATEWAYS, RELUCTANT TO GO THROUGH
See also Door, refusing to go through, Door, rushing through, Separation anxiety, Water

Puddles and boggy poached areas often form in the middle of gateways, and your horse may be reluctant to walk through these. He may try to walk round the edge and either injure himself or, if you are riding, scrape your legs against the gatepost. Improving drainage in paddock gateways, and the use of rubber matting or plastic mesh systems, will help protect the ground from the high volume of traffic, but you should spend some time also teaching your horse to move confidently over a variety of surfaces so you do not encounter difficulties when out hacking.

Your horse may also exhibit reluctance to move through a gateway if it means leaving field or stable companions behind; he may also be anxious about the gate swinging back and catching his pelvis, so make sure you open it wide enough and either keep control of it as you pass through or ask someone to hold it for you.

EXERCISE: BELLY LIFTS

If the horse is sensitive to contact around the girth area or along the belly, ask someone to hold his head. You will need a long stretchy length of bandage such as an exercise bandage.

1. You can do this exercise by yourself, or with another person. Start the lifts on the girth area beginning on the off side, since the majority of horses with this problem will have developed a negative association of someone standing next to the girth area on the near side. Pass the bandage beneath the belly, and bring the two ends up to the top of the horse's back.

2. If you are working alone, support the end of the bandage on the side furthest from you near the spine. Gently lift the bandage on the side closest to you, over a count of four. Hold the bandage in place for another count of four, and then slowly release over a count of eight. The release is the important part of the exercise. Avoid pulling the bandage tight – this exercise is more effective if you simply make contact with the horse's ribs and belly with the bandage, rather than taking up all the stretch in it.

3. Move the bandage back a couple of inches with both hands and repeat. Continue as far back as you can, watching the horse for any signs of concern.

4. If you have another person holding the other side of the bandage you can experiment by releasing alternately as well as simultaneously. Allow the horse to turn his head to look at you if he wishes. Before you start, decide between you who will drop their end of the bandage should the horse suddenly panic. However, you should find that most will start to relax and lower the neck, softening

Use a body wrap or length of stretchy bandage, and start round the girth area. Support one end of the wrap with the inside hand, and hold the other end in the outside hand. Keeping your inside hand still, lift the length of the wrap up the girth line slowly for a count of four, hold the lift for another four seconds, and then slowly release for a count of eight. It is the release that is the important part of this exercise. Remember to stay in balance yourself, and avoid lifting so high that you take all the stretch out of the wrap. If the horse is unsettled or concerned, lift less or move to another part of the body.

the eye and breathing more deeply as you do this exercise. If the horse continues to have a problem with it, a thorough veterinary examination may be required.

5. If the horse is happy with the sensation of the wrap and the lift around the girth area, you can do lifts with the girth before you actually fasten it. Remember to hold on to the saddle with one hand so that you don't pull it off the horse when you do the lifts. Fasten the girth slowly, one hole at a time, and try doing the lifts and girthing him up from the off side.

You can also do belly lifts with the girth, but remember to hold the saddle to stabilize it, and repeat the lifts a few times before slowly tightening the girth.

EXERCISE: WAND WORK

A 'wand' is a tool used in TTEAM as a way of helping to improve the horse's proprioceptive sense and co-ordination, of making contact from a safe distance if necessary, and of giving signals and cueing actions such as starting, slowing and stopping. It can be invaluable in teaching ground-work exercises, so it is worth spending some time introducing it to your horse, and learning how to handle it quietly and correctly yourself.

It is a stiff dressage stick, four foot long and with a hard button on the handle, and is used as an extension of your arm to enable you to touch the horse all over his body without compromising your safety. Using the wand to stroke the neck, chest and legs can have an amazingly calming and relaxing effect, which can be helpful in overcoming any tendency of the horse to be fidgety or spooky: it also encourages him to lower the head and neck, making it easier for him to balance.

A white whip is usually used because it is easier for the horse to see, but if he appears nervous of this colour, use a black or brown one instead. If your horse is whip shy, work through the exercises described in that section before trying this exercise.

Before you start, practise using the wand on another person to get a feel for it before trying it on a horse – a person can also give you valuable feedback regarding your technique.

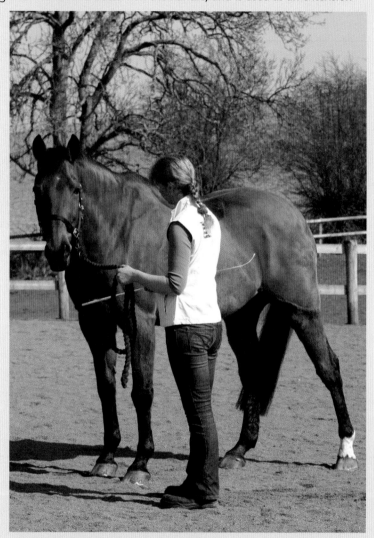

Teaching a horse to accept and enjoy contact over every part of his body is integral to overall health and well being. Most horses can tolerate contact down the underside of the neck and chest. Introduce the wand by stroking the horse with the button end first to minimize any concerns he may have.

1. Working on the left side of his body, hold the leadrope close to the headcollar with a soft contact. Hold the wand in your right hand like a sword, button end up and keeping your hand relaxed, as a tight grip will inhibit the co-ordination, delicacy and precision with which you use it.

2. Start by stroking the front of the chest with the wand, as this is the least threatening place to start. If the horse is settled, slide out on the leadline and turn the wand round and repeat the stroking on the chest with the full length of the wand. If he remains calm, use a series of slow, graceful, downward and slightly forward sweeps, following the

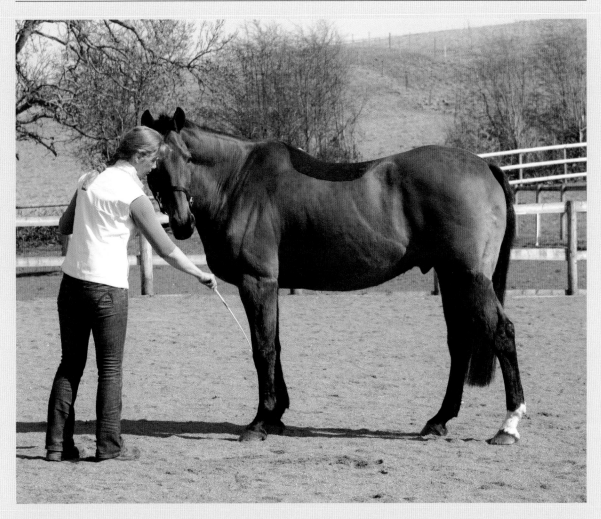

Once the horse is happy being stroked with the button end of the wand, you can try stroking him down his front legs with the full length of the wand. Keep your hand contact soft, and move your body as you stroke to keep the movement fluid and relaxing. Gripping the wand will increase the pressure, and bracing in your own body will make the movement more erratic, which may alarm the horse.

contours of the horse's body, down the chest and down the front of the forelegs. The pressure should be positive and firm enough to make contact without tickling, but not so strong as to cause discomfort.

3. If your horse is not showing any anxiety about this, use the wand to stroke the whole underside of his neck, progressing slowly and steadily downwards to the front of the chest again, continuing to work down the front legs, right down to the ends of the hooves.

4. Progress to stroking the wand all over his body, along his shoulders, back, quarters, neck and down each of his legs, going with the lie of his coat. Remember to keep your movements steady and rhythmical, avoiding any abrupt movements; if he shows any concern or tries to move away from you, return to working on areas he is comfortable about, or give him a break.

5. Change sides and repeat the work from the off side.

Suggested exercises: Labyrinth, Narrow Spaces, Sliding Numnahs, Stroking the Line, Walking over Plastic, Work over Different Surfaces

GETTING UP, DIFFICULTY IN
See Lying down

GIRTHING ISSUES
See also Cold backed, Grooming issues, Saddling issues

Many horses have girthing issues, and may display their concern by blowing out their belly, lifting a leg, grinding their teeth, biting and so on when the girth is tightened. As well as addressing any possible source of pain caused through poor saddle fit, or negative associations with being ridden – such as, for example, poor rider posture – breaking down the girthing process and changing his expectation can help a horse overcome this problem. You may also need to invest in a new girth that is padded and has elastic on both sides, and to pay attention to where you put the saddle, because it is often placed too far forward on the horse's back.

Some horses that have never been backed show sensitivity around the girth area, especially those that are (or were) croup high, as this unlevel posture can create tension around the back of the shoulders. It is obviously very important from a safety point of view – and far nicer for the horse – if this is addressed before a girth or lungeing roller is introduced.

Suggested exercises: Belly Lifts, Ear Work, Forelock Slides, Lick of the Cow's Tongue, Tail Work

GROOMING ISSUES
See also Aggression, Clipping, Cowkicking, Feet, picking up, Head shy, Standing still, Whip shy

A horse which is difficult to groom may have become so because of rough and careless grooming in the past causing discomfort, or if he is apprehensive about people due to lack of, or limited, human contact. In most cases, however, it is linked to areas of sensitivity in the horse's body, and the horse may have been punished in the past for exhibiting his concern. This problem is often associated with issues with being saddled and/or rugged, so it is important to check that equipment and rugs fit comfortably.

Start by running the flat of your hand gently over the horse's body, starting at the poll and working along the body. Remember to check both sides, and avoid shouting at your horse if he moves away, lifts a leg or attempts to bite. You may notice that the appearance of the eye changes when you touch a specific part of the body, or that he bites the leadrope. All these are signs that your horse is uncomfortable, whether it is because he is sensitive or has an expectation of discomfort.

With patience you can overcome this problem. Try using a sheepskin mitt, and stroke gently with it all over your horse's body to change his expectation of grooming. Once he is happy to be stroked all over in this way, experiment with soft rubber groomers or soft bodybrushes, and use products that help to loosen dirt and grease without resorting to rigorous grooming with a stiff bristled brush. You need to take your time, and remember that grooming should be a beneficial exercise for both of you. You can also try laying a damp, warm towel over his body (taking into account the weather at the time), or using heat packs to do some body work (*see* Chapter 5) prior to grooming to increase circulation and reduce tension in the muscles and skin.

With a horse that is wary of any physical contact you may have to abandon any idea of grooming until he has developed more confidence about the presence of people and being touched all over his body. This can be achieved by using a 'wand', which will enable you to initiate physical contact from a safe distance.

Once the horse is relaxed and accepting of the contact of the wand, you can add a sheepskin mitt or roll a bandage around the end, which will give a different feel, and acts as a halfway step between using the wand and actually touching him with your hand. When you do reach this point, stroke him using the back of your hand or with the sheepskin mitt, and gradually you will be able to progress to using soft brushes. Don't try to rush the process, and bear in mind that, especially in the early stages, developing confidence is of more importance than making him clean.

Suggested exercises: Forelock Circles and Slides, Jellyfish Jiggles, Tail Work, Wand Work, ZigZag

HALTING
See Standing still

HEADSHAKING
See also Snatching at reins

Ranging from small, mild twitches to extreme and violent movements that can make the horse unsafe to ride, headshaking is frequently accompanied by excessive snorting and frantic rubbing of the nose against a foreleg, the ground, a handler or anything else handy.

Headshaking is a medical condition rather than a behavioural one. There are numerous theories as to the cause, including nerve pain caused by damaged sensory nerves in the head, allergic reactions, hypersensitivity to ultraviolet light, a form of neuralgia causing shooting pains in the nose, mouth and dental problems, parasites and hay seeds in the ears,

If the browband is too tight the headpiece will restrict movement through the ears and increase pressure around the poll.

sinus and throat problems. You should check bit and bridle fit so that these at least can be eliminated.

While it is a seasonal problem for many horses – around 50 per cent are affected between March and October, with symptoms improving dramatically or vanishing altogether during the winter – others headshake all year round. Exercise, heat, wind and sunlight all appear to either exacerbate or trigger the problem: keeping a diary noting what things seem to make it worse may help in pinpointing contributory factors. There may be a number of triggers rather than a single specific one.

Ask your vet to examine the horse, and discuss the options available with him. Various drugs and surgical techniques are available, although success is variable; some people have reported that alternative therapies

EXERCISE: SHOULDER PRESSES

This Connected Riding exercise encourages the horse to release the shoulder and base of the neck, while you support him through the movement. It helps him bend and soften through the neck and to lengthen through the top line, so can help horses that find it hard to work up and into the bridle. It also helps the horse to open and release through the ribcage, reducing gait irregularity and improving hind-limb engagement, and is useful in establishing lateral movement.

1. Start off working from the left side, as this is likely to be easier for the horse. Stand near the shoulder facing towards his side, holding the leadrope in your left hand and close to the headcollar. Make a soft fist with your right hand and place it against the fleshy muscle in the middle of the shoulder, approximately two to three fist widths back from the point of the shoulder, depending on the size of the horse.
2. Place your feet slightly apart, with your right foot slightly further forward, keeping your knees and hips slightly flexed and soft. Slowly press your right fist into the shoulder while at the same time slowly rotating your body to the left. This rotation is important as it helps you to create a supportive movement through the horse's shoulder, as opposed to simply pushing him over: you want him to release into the movement, not push back into your hand in resistance.

Start by practising this exercise while the horse is standing to check for any sensitivity. Support the line in the outside hand, and place the back of your hand in the middle of his shoulder. Slowly rotate your body away from the horse to ensure that the movement comes through from your feet as opposed to simply pushing into the horse. Hold the press for one or two seconds, then slowly rotate back to your starting place. You should feel the horse softening and slightly flexing his neck.

3. Hold this position for a moment and watch the horse's reaction. Slowly rotate your body back to the right, releasing the pressure on his shoulder as you do so. It is this release that is the most important part of the exercise as it gives the horse the opportunity to respond to the movement and to soften and adjust his posture accordingly. Pay attention to your left hand, and remember to think 'up' with it; this helps you to keep the contact light and connected, and minimizes the chances of you inadvertently pulling the horse's head down. Note that thinking 'up' doesn't mean you need to actually lift your hand.

4. Repeat this exercise a few times, then switch to the other side. Note whether the horse is more accepting of the shoulder presses on a particular side, and whether the amount of release is equal on both sides.

5. This exercise can be done while the horse is standing or walking. If doing it while on the move, angle your body to allow you to walk alongside him without being trodden on. Remember to still rotate your body slightly away from the horse to initiate the press. You can also try this exercise with two leadropes, taking a soft contact on the outside line with the hand doing the presses on the shoulder.

6. Most horses enjoy the opportunity to release old bracing patterns through this exercise, but if your horse is crooked, stiff or sore through the shoulders he may find it difficult at first. To help him gain the most from it, make sure your fist is in the soft, fleshy part of the shoulder, and experiment with the pressure of the press, making the movement minimal if he shows any signs of discomfort or concern.

Ask the horse to walk forwards, and use the same movement as before. Repeat this a few times, and then let your horse walk on for a few strides. This helps to increase stride length and free up a tight neck and back. It can also be done with the aid of a helper once the horse is under saddle.

including homoeopathy, herbal supplements, acupuncture and osteopathy have helped. Often it is a case of managing the problem rather than curing it: wetting the hay, stabling during the day and turning out at night, and the use of fine mesh nose nets and other facial coverings can all help in reducing the severity of the symptoms.

Some headshakers benefit from the TTEAM body-work and ground-work exercises aimed at lowering stress levels and releasing tension, in particular through the neck and withers – though this will, of course, depend on the reasons why the headshaking occurs. It is imperative that the handler's safety is a priority: the horse may involuntarily strike out with a front leg, or headshake so violently that it causes injury to the handler.

HEAD SHY
See also Bridle, difficult to

Rough handling or abrupt, sudden movements by the handler can lead to the horse becoming concerned about having his head touched. Ear and dental pain, tension around the poll, and a poorly fitting bridle can also be responsible, so ask your vet and an equine dental technician to check for physical problems, and check bridle and bit fit.

Be careful and patient when grooming the face, using soft brushes or a sheepskin mitt, or your fingers. As well as trying the exercises suggested below, using TTouches (*see* Chapter 5) can be helpful in creating relaxation. Stand at the side and gradually work towards touching difficult spots, but don't force the issue if the horse starts to show concern: move your hand back to an area where he is happy to allow contact. Continue doing TTouches there for a while, and then slowly approach the difficult place again. It may take time to regain trust and confidence; you may find it helpful to try doing this work while the horse is wearing a body wrap.

Don't attempt to handle the head while the horse is tied up, or to restrain him strongly with the leadrope, as restricting movement may cause him to become more anxious. Always approach from the side – touching his face without warning may startle him if he doesn't see your hand coming due to the 'blind' spot directly in front of his muzzle.

Suggested exercises: Body Wraps, Ear Work, Forelock work, Mouth Work, Tail Work

HIGH HEADED
See Outline, Bit evasions

JOGGING
See also Balance, Bit evasions, Separation anxiety, Snatching at the reins

Often accompanied by snatching at the reins, jogging may be due to discomfort from an ill-fitting bridle, bit or saddle, or physical problems in the mouth, ears, back and/or limbs. Cold and windy weather and also freshness can be responsible, especially if the horse is under-exercised, in which case it will usually cease as he settles into his work. Many horses will also quicken their steps when heading towards home, and may keep breaking into a jog.

Pushing the horse on too fast so that he is out of balance, and it is beyond his ability to lengthen his stride, will also cause him to jog; and if you are riding with longer striding horses his jogging may be linked to anxiety about being left behind. The rider's posture and aid application can also lie at the heart of the problem, so check for over-restriction with the hands, overstrong leg aids, gripping up with the lower legs, and poor posture generally.

The short, bumpy jogging stride can be jarring on the horse's legs as well as tiring and uncomfortable for both rider and horse, so it is worthwhile making the effort to remedy the problem rather than living with it. Poor balance will contribute to jogging, so using a Balance Rein can be especially helpful; it will help in rebalancing and steadying the horse through the whole of his body while simultaneously helping to prevent the instinctive reaction of tightening or pulling back on the reins, which then creates a vicious circle of horse and rider both battling for control.

If jogging is due to excitement, the balance rein will also encourage lowering of the head and neck, helping to change the horse's posture from the high-headed one often adopted at such times to a calmer, more relaxed frame. Slow pelvic rotations left and right can also be helpful because they stop the rider from bracing, release tension in the back, and encourage the horse to soften through the neck.

Suggested exercises: Balance Rein, Floating Forwards, Leg Circles, Mouth Work, Rotating the Pelvis, Shoulder Presses, Sternum Lifts, Stroking the Reins, Tail Work

JUMPING, BUCKING ON LANDING
See also Bucking

This behaviour is more often due to reasons of discomfort than high spirits, which might include hitting a pole, the rider getting left behind or sitting up too early, or back problems. Limb pain can also be responsible, or if the horse makes either a particularly athletic effort or an awkward jump which causes a twinge through the back and pelvic region.

Saddle fit should be carefully checked: even though the pommel may give adequate clearance while the horse is working on the flat, the front arch may press on the withers as the horse lands over a fence. The rider should check their leg position too, as some horses will object if it slips back too far as they jump.

Suggested exercises: Balance Rein, Belly Lifts, Caterpillar, Tail Work, ZigZag

JUMPING, REFUSING
See also Jumping, bucking, Nappiness, Rushing

Refusing a jump is one of the commonest jumping problems, and there can be numerous reasons for this happening: overfacing the horse, bad presentation, changes in light conditions, fatigue, concern about the appearance of the fence, deep or slippery going, nappiness, fear of pain, or a previous bad experience.

If a horse starts refusing regularly when he has previously been jumping confidently, however, physical pain should be the first thing to consider. As well as having him thoroughly checked over, bear in mind that saddlery, over-bitting, poor rider position and hard ground can be frequent causes of discomfort. A brewing foot abscess or changes to the bony structures to the hoof may also be responsible.

Over-jumping can lead to sourness and refusing, especially if the fences or gymnastic exercises chosen are constantly highly demanding. Nor should the rider's technique be overlooked either, as nervousness and lack of commitment, over-restriction with the rein contact, holding the breath, and over-strong riding are just as likely to be responsible for causing the problem.

Where a horse is refusing due to loss of confidence following a bad experience, it may be necessary to return to basics, using polework before gradually reintroducing small and simple fences. Where a refusal has occurred due to poor presentation or uncertainty about the appearance of fence, always reduce the size and degree of difficulty before making a second attempt, so as to rebuild the confidence of both horse and rider.

Suggested exercises: Balance Rein, Deep Breathing, Leg Circles, Pick up Sticks, Solo Polework, Tail Work, ZigZag

EXERCISE: THE ZIGZAG

Polework exercises are excellent for developing confidence, balance and co-ordination, and can be set up in many ways to add variety to your horse's work, as well as helping to resolve any specific issues he may have. This particular exercise can be performed either in hand or mounted, and will improve engagement of the quarters, increase the range of movement through the shoulders, and encourage lateral flexion through the ribcage. It is a great way to prepare your horse for jumping fences at angles or meeting arrowhead-type cross-country fences, and can also be used to help introduce poles to youngsters or spooky horses.

1. Place four poles flat on the ground so they form a zigzag pattern, with the ends of the poles lying at right angles to each other, but with a gap left between them.
2. Walk around outside the poles – if your horse is very spooky he may find even this difficult. If you are leading him, keep yourself between him and the poles so he does not step sideways into you. As his confidence grows, ask him to walk towards the gap in the centre of the ZigZag. Halt just before the gap, in the middle of it, and just after it to encourage him to rebalance and assess matters. If he shows concern about the poles, make the gaps between them wider.

If the horse is worried about poles on the ground, set up a single line of zigzag poles and walk the horse past them.

3. Once your horse is comfortable with this, gradually close up the gaps between the poles until they are finally touching. Ask someone to assist you so you don't make your horse anxious by trying to shift poles about whilst still holding him.
4. Walk towards one of the arrowheads formed by the poles so that the point is facing away from you; halt just in front of it before then asking him to walk on over it.
5. Next, progress to walking over one of the arrowheads, approaching so that the point of the V faces towards you instead. Remember to approach from different directions, and if on foot, lead from both the left and the right side too; change just one element of an exercise and it will become a whole new learning experience for the horse.

6. Next, try walking over each of the poles individually, turning left and right over them; the series of S-shaped bends your horse moves through as he does this will help free up his ribcage.

7. Try leading your horse in a straight line through the length of the ZigZag so that he crosses each pole at an angle. As the distances will vary and the poles are not met square on, it will teach him to focus on what he is doing, and increase his co-ordination and awareness of how he is moving his legs and positioning his feet.

8. The exercise can be further varied by creating a double ZigZag, adding a second set of poles lying parallel to the first, to create an avenue which can be walked through or crossed in the same ways as before.

Lead him through the gap in the poles so that he becomes accustomed to walking between them. You can widen the gap if he is really worried and build up his confidence over several sessions.

As his confidence grows, narrow the gap between the ends of the poles to encourage him to step over the poles. You can ride this exercise too, to help give you and your horse a visual aid. Note whether he steps to the left or right of the arrowhead, and practise either in hand or under saddle until he is walking over the centre in a straight line.

Leading the horse through zigzag poles helps to develop confidence and balance. Ask the horse to halt before each turn, and note whether he finds it easier to turn in a particular direction. You can also ride through the zigzags to improve your own co-ordination and concentration.

JUMPING, RUNNING OUT

See also Jumping, refusing, Rushing

A horse may run out to the side of a fence for the same reasons as he may refuse, although most frequently poor presentation is to blame, presenting the horse at too acute an angle. While jumping fences at an angle may be something you will need to teach your horse for competition purposes, it should be introduced gradually, and over small and simple fences initially. If this is a common event, look for a pattern, as it may be that the horse only runs out when approaching the jump from a specific direction.

Suggested exercises: Labyrinth, Leg Circles, Shoulder Presses, Solo Polework, Wither Rocking, ZigZag

---

EXERCISE: THE LABYRINTH

The horse can be ridden or led through this simple exercise, and the results can be outstanding. The purpose of it is to help the horse become less one-sided, developing greater flexibility through the neck and ribcage, and giving him the ability to use his hindquarters more effectively. This exercise also has a very calming effect on most horses.

The aim is to teach the horse to walk slowly through the pattern formed by the poles, halting approximately one stride before making each turn, so that he is encouraged to think about how to organize his body. This helps him learn to co-ordinate himself more quickly than if he walks straight through the poles without stopping. Horses that are out of balance will tend to rush through the exercise and may find it hard to stop at first; those that are too nervous to walk between the poles initially should start with an easier exercise such as the ZigZag (see previous problem).

For a basic Labyrinth you will need eight 12ft poles laid out as shown in the photo. The width between the poles will vary depending on the size and balance of the horse: some may need to have them set wide apart due to fear or stiffness in the body, but you should see an improvement quite quickly, enabling you to work towards placing the poles approximately four feet (1m) apart.

Set out the poles in the configuration as shown, and lead the horse through the exercise. Some horses panic and rush: if this is the case do not try to force him round, but take him out and try again. Once your horse is confident walking between the poles, ask him to halt one stride before the end of each pole. Ask him to walk and turn round each end. The halt is important as it teaches him how to organize his body and engage his hindquarters.

1. If working alone, start by leading your horse from the near side as you will probably both find this easiest. (If he is out of balance and crowds you, use the exercise

Homing Pigeon, but make sure that you communicate clearly with your assistant, and that neither one of you gets left behind through each turn. The person on the inside will need to steady the horse, while the person on the outside steps forward before the horse makes the turn.)

2. Lead the horse slowly through the Labyrinth, asking him to halt before each turn. Make sure you stay in front of the horse's nose, and give him plenty of time and space in which to stop. To prepare for a transition to halt give a gentle ask-and-release signal on the leadrope, and bring the wand back towards the horse's chest. Use your voice and then, as you say 'Whoooaa', reach across his chest with the wand and touch the opposite point of his shoulder. This encourages the horse to keep his hindquarters straight while stopping. Stroke down the underside of his neck and down his chest and forelegs with the wand to help him to balance in the halt, and to stay relaxed. Note whether he habitually halts with a particular leg forward or back.

3. If the horse cannot stop when you first ask him, or is concerned about standing between poles, you can lead him straight on, crossing over them, and then try again. While he is moving forwards, use the wand as an extension of your arm to help guide him through the Labyrinth; you may need to step outside the poles yourself to allow him room to turn.

4. It doesn't matter if the horse cannot complete the Labyrinth exercise straightaway, and you may both need to practise it many times before the exercise becomes more fluent. Lead him through the Labyrinth from both directions. You may find that he can bend one way and not the other, or that he becomes stuck on the turns and

You can also use the Labyrinth as walk-over poles, and raise alternate ends of them to add variety to the exercise.

moves around the end of the poles with his forelegs whilst swivelling on his hind legs. You may also note that he can cross one hind leg to the midline on the turn but not the other. All this will relate to any schooling difficulties that you have, and will help to teach him a more efficient and balanced way of moving.

5. The Labyrinth exercise can also highlight other problems. If the horse can negotiate his way round the Labyrinth with ease in hand, but becomes stuck when saddled or ridden through the exercise, you may need to address the fit of the saddle and/or your own posture and aids.

As the horse must really concentrate when working through the Labyrinth, it can be a useful exercise for settling him if he is anxious. It can also be used to help a horse overcome issues with spooking, as you can add different objects around the edges of the arena: he will gain greater confidence by working through the Labyrinth than if you simply tried to walk him past them. It will also help to improve your own balance and co-ordination.

JUMPING, RUSHING FENCES
See also Balance, Over-excitable, Rushing

Rushing fences is more often due to anxiety than enthusiasm, although a bold horse may use speed to compensate for lack of scope, strength and suppleness. Where a rider's inexperience or his own anxiety causes him to ride the horse forwards too fast, it can become an established habit. As with refusing and running out, pain as a cause or contributory factor should be looked into and remedied as appropriate, after which a return to basics, schooling on the flat and using polework is advisable before building up to working over fences again.

Suggested exercises: Balance Rein, Deep Breathing, Floating Forwards, Neutral Pelvis, The Labyrinth, ZigZag

KICKING
See also Aggression, Bullying, Cowkicking, Doors, kicking at

From a horse's point of view, kicking is usually a very effective way of getting rid of, or deterring, anything perceived as threatening or causing pain or fear, whether this is another horse, a dog or a person. Many horses that kick are tight through the hamstrings and tight in the tail, and exercises aimed at releasing tension will be of benefit, although care should be taken when working around the hindquarters.

If a horse is startled it may also kick out defensively, so regardless of how placid a horse may be, or how well you may think you know him, always approach from the side when greeting him so he can see you before you touch him. Speak to him when working around him in the stable so he always knows where you are, and when picking up a hind foot don't make a sudden grab for it, but stroke a hand from his shoulder, along his back to the quarters and down the length of the leg to the hoof.

Never ignore a kick threat, when the horse purposefully swings his quarters towards you: always take it very seriously, and never respond with force which is likely to turn the threat into a reality. If he presents his quarters to you when entering the stable or catching him in the field, encourage him to approach you head first. Use food as a lure if necessary, and put a headcollar on so you can prevent him from swinging his quarters towards you again. You will need to work out what the horse is concerned about – it may be the way he is ridden or handled, or that he is insufficiently acquainted with people or has suffered abuse at their hands. Re-establishing his trust may take time and patient work: the exercise Wand Work may help to re-initiate a calm contact with the horse, while enabling you to keep a safe distance from his back legs. Be careful of his front legs, too, as a horse which is highly concerned may instead strike out with a front foot: position yourself to the side, not directly in front of him.

Some horses lack confidence with other horses, or fear them coming too close: keep to the rear when riding out in groups, and warn others to keep their distance when working in the school. Traditionally a red ribbon is tied to the top of the tail of a horse liable to kick when out in public. It should go without saying that a horse known to kick should not be turned out in the field with others.

Some horses will kick out or buck when first turned out in the field through impatience and sheer high spirits. Always keep yourself safe by taking such a horse through the gate and then turning its head back to face you. Leave the gate slightly ajar, release the horse and slip through the gap while he is turning round, so you are never in the way of his back feet.

Suggested exercises: Ear Work, Forelock Pulls, Wand Work

LAZINESS
See also Balance, Crookedness, Leading, Outline, Standing still, Stiffness

Numerous factors can contribute to perceived 'laziness', including physical problems such as arthritis, anaemia, sore feet, ill-fitting saddlery and dental issues; or maybe the horse is lacking in strength, suppleness or fitness, or perhaps doesn't understand the leg aids. Boredom can also play a part, and if his work lacks in variety the horse may simply switch off, becoming slow to respond. Make sure his feed is sufficient to meet his energy requirements. The way in which the horse moves can also be part of the problem: if he is crooked or on the forehand, free forward movement will be impeded, as will over-severe bitting, and/or too strong a rein.

If your horse doesn't respond instantly when asked to move forwards he is not necessarily being idle, unresponsive or disobedient. It can take a few seconds for the message to filter through from brain to body, and the less well balanced he is, the longer it will take him to respond to your request. Co-ordinating four legs and a body weighing in the region of half a ton is not the easiest thing to do, and especially if he's learning to do something in a new way, it may take extra time for him to work out how to organize himself.

EXERCISE: PROMISE ROPE
If your horse is inclined to be nervous or spooky, the Promise Wrap exercise (*see* problem Standing Still) may be more appropriate; others may respond better to this one, the Promise Rope. As with the wrap, the rope encourages engagement of the quarters and elevation of the horse's frame through the withers. Use a length of soft rope – available from climbing or marine stores – and attach and introduce it in exactly the same way as the Promise Wrap.

Once the horse is accustomed to the feel of the rope, tying a knot at the back helps to weight it and give it a little more swing against the quarters. You may need to experiment a little to find the right height to suit the horse, but ideally it should sit between the hock and the point of the buttock at the top of the gaskin. The rope should hang in a light, rather than snug contact, and must not drop over the hocks.

How long you leave the rope on for and how often you use it depends on the individual – it may be an isolated occasion, or used during several consecutive sessions and thereafter as felt necessary. Remember to keep sessions short, because if you do too much your horse may feel sore from overworking unaccustomed muscles.

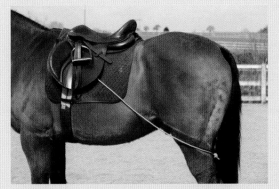

Follow the steps for attaching the promise wrap, and tie a knot in the middle of the rope to give more weight to the line.

Make sure that the knot is in the middle of the hind legs when the horse is at rest.

Applying stronger leg aids can often have the reverse effect to that intended, causing him to brace through the belly and ribcage muscles, which will inhibit forward movement. Leaning back with the upper body and/or driving strongly with the seat will also be punishing and counter-productive as it can cause the horse's back to hollow, with subsequent loss of engagement from behind – it can also cause actual physical damage to the back. Use the Pelvic Rotations and Floating Forward exercises to encourage forward movement and release tension through the ribs and back. Pause between each request: use verbal cues to help encourage him, and bear in mind that he may be slow to respond if your signals aren't clear, are contradictory, or interfere with his balance.

Suggested exercises: Balance Rein, Dingo, Floating Forwards, Leg Circles, Neutral Pelvis, Promise Rope, Rotating the Pelvis, Shoulder Presses, Sternum Lifts, Tail Work

LEADING, CROWDING
See also Balance, Crookedness, Leading issues, Separation anxiety, Standing still

Leading the horse from a position near his head rather than by his shoulder will make it easier to avoid him should he step sideways into you. Spending time teaching him to walk just a few steps at a time and then halting again, whilst using the wand in a gentle fanning movement to encourage him to keep his distance will help; the Homing Pigeon exercise (*see* below, Leading Issues) can also be useful in teaching him to balance and move more independently.

Horses that crowd you or seem unable to walk in a straight line when being led may also be suffering from insecurity and lack of confidence and/or concentration, as well as having poor balance and proprioceptive sense, so exercises such as polework and moving over different surfaces will be helpful.

Suggested exercises: Body Wraps, Homing Pigeon, Labyrinth, Leg Circles, Raised Polework, Solo polework, Work over Different Surfaces, Walking over Plastic, Wand Work, Wither Rocking, ZigZag

LEADING, HANGING BACK
See also Balance, Laziness, Leading issues, Separation anxiety, Tying up

If your horse hangs back or runs back, or goes into freeze (*see* Chapter 1), this generally means that he is confused, or anxious about something – he may have heard or seen something that alarms him – or he may be concerned about leaving his friends. Pulling his head down, trying to drag him forwards, or hanging on to him can trigger a more defensive and possibly dangerous reaction. If he is constantly sluggish and reluctant to move forwards, check for physical problems.

If he is hanging back, use the exercise called 'Dingo' below (but only if you have already taught it to him), or wait for a moment and then try the exercise Stroking the Line (*see* the problem 'Nappiness'). You might also try asking your horse to step slightly away from you if he has gone into freeze, in order to help him unlock his neck which is likely to be braced, or stroking him down his chest and front legs with the wand to help him feel his body and legs.

If he is running back, go with him, as pulling on his head will usually send him backwards even faster. In all our years of working with horses we have found that the majority will only go back a few paces if allowed the freedom to do so, and you can then 'Stroke the Line', or stroke him with the wand, to help him settle and relax and therefore release the tension in his neck.

Suggested exercises: Caterpillar, Dingo, Stroking the Line, Walking the S, Wand Work, Wither Rocking

EXERCISE: DINGO

This exercise can be used for horses that lack impulsion, scuff their hind feet, are reluctant to walk forwards, or rush, and those that are reluctant to load or walk into a stable or through a gateway. Make sure you have first read the sections 'Leading issues', 'Wand work' and 'Whip shy', and have completed the exercises successfully.

1. Attach the lead line to the side of the headcollar, and hold it in your outside hand. Fold the line over the palm of your hand with your hand up by the headcollar so you are facing towards the horse as shown in the photograph. Hold the wand in your other hand.

2. Stroke the horse along his back from the withers towards the croup, repeating this two or three

LEFT: *Steady the head by holding the line near the headcollar, and stroke the wand along the horse's back.*

BELOW: *Give a signal forward on the line and bounce the wand gently on the croup with a forward motion. Avoid gripping the wand and keep your hand soft; this will prevent you from stinging the horse with the wand.*

times. If your horse starts to move forwards, ask him to steady with a gentle ask-and-release signal on the lead line. If he panics, he is not ready for this exercise and you will need to go back to the Wand Work exercises.

3. If he is calm, give him a light forward ask-and-release signal on the lead line, followed by two light taps with the wand on the croup, keeping your palm soft and your wrist and arm relaxed. If you tighten your grip on the wand or carry tension through your arm the wand will sting your horse, which is not the point of the exercise – the aim is to teach him to engage his hindquarters and to increase his mind/body awareness, not to make him rocket forwards.

4. You can only walk a few steps in this position as you are facing the wrong way. Bring the wand past his body and stop him with a signal on the chest. If he starts bowling on, swap the lead line back into both hands, and turn yourself so you are facing forwards in the direction of movement. Hold the wand in the hand furthest away from the horse, and use it on the front of his chest to help cue the halt as described in the section 'Leading issues'.

LEADING ISSUES

See also Balance, Clumsiness, Leading, crowding, Leading, hanging back, Loading, Outline, Whip shy

Horses can be difficult to lead for a number of reasons: for example, they may never have been taught to lead correctly, may have been forcefully handled, have an incorrect posture which makes it hard for them to maintain their own balance, or perhaps have dental problems that cause discomfort.

A variety of TTEAM leading exercises will be beneficial, although you should first eliminate any possible causes of physical discomfort. By teaching a horse to lead quietly but freely in hand, the obvious benefit is that you will be

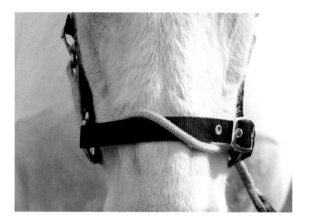

Thread it through the ring on the opposite side of the headcollar, passing it through the ring from the inside. Run the line up the side of the headcollar, and attach it to the ring by the cheek bone.

making life easier, less stressful and safer for both of you – but it goes further than this. Your horse's behaviour, posture and movement in hand will all be amplified when under saddle, so any time spent teaching the horse to maintain his own self-carriage when led will improve every aspect of his ridden work. Improving posture from the ground will also boost self-control and self-confidence, so plays an important part in helping him overcome any concerns.

Safety is of paramount importance, so if the horse is strong, wear gloves, and if necessary, enlist the help of another experienced person. If he barges and steps on your feet, remember that this is not a sign of dominance but of poor balance, so avoid shouting at, or smacking him. If a horse is really challenging to lead, practise with an easier horse first, so you can refine your leading position and use of the wand without worrying about the horse.

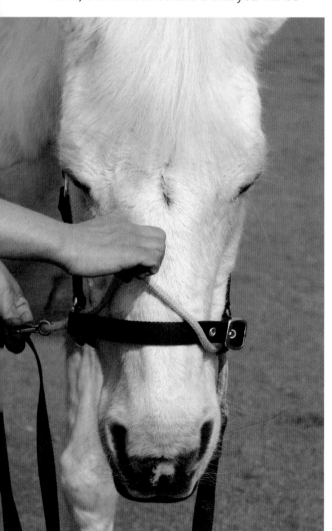

Start by attaching a TTEAM soft line by threading the clip through the ring at the side of the noseband. Drop the line down through the ring, then pass it up and over the noseband. This prevents the line from tightening round the nasal bone.

Equipment

The TTEAM leading exercises aim to teach the horse how to organize his whole body efficiently, and the TTEAM lead line and 'wand' are invaluable tools.

Attach a TTEAM soft lead as shown in the photographs. If you are unable to purchase a soft lead you could use a length of thin climbing rope instead; even clipping a regular rope to the side of the headcollar as opposed to under the jaw will enable you to give a more subtle signal on the lead line. This is particularly important with a horse that is high-headed and/or sensitive around the poll, because like this, pressure is reduced on the area which can cause him to raise his head higher. Leading the horse from the side of the headcollar also gives you more choices in your hand position when working through some of the other exercises in this book.

Positioning Yourself

Riders spend many hours trying to improve their horse's movement under saddle, and then undo much of what is achieved by reinforcing his poor posture through habitually leading him from the near side, and by positioning themselves between his eye and shoulder. These two traditional practices create an unbalanced posture, with the horse loading his weight on the near fore and bracing through the neck.

Clipping the leadrope to the side of the headcollar or using a TTEAM soft lead looped over the noseband helps to teach the horse to walk calmly in self carriage. You can use a schooling stick as an extension of your arm to ask the horse to slow. Stay in front of the horse's nose to avoid pulling back, which will bring the horse on to the inside foreleg and create uneven muscling in the neck.

Instead, stand to the side, but slightly ahead of the horse's nose: this will enable you to keep his neck as straight as possible, and he will be able to see the wand more clearly. Hold the line in two hands, with it lying across the palm of the hand nearest the headcollar. Keep your hand relaxed, as holding the line with a closed fist will create more tension on it and trigger further bracing in the horse's head and neck. Hold the wand in the outside hand and make sure that the end of the line is not looped around your hand or fingers. Position yourself so the wand is level with your horse's chest, but angled away from him, as opposed to crossing his path.

TTEAM practitioners teach horses to be led from both sides as this helps to create evenness, but some horses find being led from the off side challenging. Changing just one thing can change everything for the horse, and if he is crooked in the neck, altering the neck position by leading from the off side may even cause him to panic. If he does show concern, make the transition to doing this easier by teaching the Homing Pigeon leading exercise (*see* opposite). Make sure that the lead line is not looped over your fingers or hand; if the line is long, make a fold in it.

Using the Wand

The 'wand' is a 4ft (122cm) long dressage schooling stick, which is usually white in colour as this makes it more easily visible to the horse. It is used as an extension of your arm to help give the horse cues as to how you want him to organize his body. It is important that you read and work through the Wand Work (*see*

To ask for a halt, keep your feet moving as you take the wand towards the horse's chest. If he finds it hard to slow or stop, rotate your body towards the horse and touch his opposite shoulder with the wand. You need to be up in front of his nose and slightly to the side in order for this to be effective.

Grooming issues) and 'Whip, fear of' exercises first, as many spooky horses, or those that barge and lack spatial awareness, may be concerned by the wand.

● When asking for a halt, move the wand in one slow up-and-down movement about three feet (90cm) in front of the horse's nose, keeping your wrist soft but straight and allowing the movement to come from your whole arm. Move the wand towards his chest to encourage him to move his centre of gravity back, saying the words 'Aaaa' and 'Whoooooa' as you do so, and giving a gentle ask-and-release signal on the lead line. The release part of the signal is important, as maintaining tension on the line will encourage him to pull. Remember that the aim is to teach him to stop through the body.

EXERCISE: HOMING PIGEON

This is an exercise where the horse learns to work between two people. This can be a valuable tool when working with difficult horses or those that are so crooked they cannot help but fall through the shoulder and into the handler. It is also a useful stepping stone to teaching a horse to be led from both sides, as leading from the off side can be confusing for many horses if they are unaccustomed to it. Before starting, it is important that you decide which person is going to give the cues to start and stop – if you both use your wands and give signals on the lead line, the horse will become confused and might panic.

Your assistant will be positioned on the opposite side of the horse, and assuming that you will be making all the decisions, will be in the role of 'co-pilot' – not giving any signals, but helping the horse to balance if necessary by taking a contact on their lead line if you ask them to. It's essential that when they do this, you 'give' at the same time, avoiding any contact on your lead line, so the horse isn't stuck in the middle of a tug of war. Remember that you will need to keep your assistant fully informed about the direction you want to go in, and when you are going to ask the horse to start and stop. It's a good idea to practise with a quiet horse so you learn to communicate clearly and to work as a team.

You should both be positioned far enough forward that you can see each other just in front of the horse's nose. Hold both wands in front of his muzzle, and as you ask the horse to move forwards, open them both out to the front. When you want to stop, you give the signals to halt while your co-pilot keeps their wand quietly in front of the horse to help him keep his balance.

For safety, your assistant's lead line should not be clipped on to the headcollar, but instead a length of soft rope should be looped through the side ring of the noseband and both ends held: like this it can then be quickly and easily slipped free by releasing one end if necessary.

Both handlers need to be forward in front of the horse's nose, and only one handler should be giving the signals with the lead line. If both handlers give signals on the lead line the horse will become confused and may panic, so good communication is essential with this exercise.

● Give him time to respond as he has to hear your voice, process the visual cue and organize his body accordingly. Keep your own feet walking until the horse actually halts – many of us automatically stop the moment we want our horse to stop, which immediately pulls him off balance. The speed with which he responds (or doesn't!) will be indicative of his balance and his ability to organize his body. You can also do this to ask him to slow down if he is starting to rush – or you can try lowering the wand so that he walks into it with his front legs, provided it is safe to do so.

● If he cannot stop, open out your arm again, repeat the movement and the verbal cue, and this time tap him gently on the point of the shoulder furthest away from you.

● If he still cannot stop, move your inside hand up the line closer to the headcollar and try again, turning his head slightly away from you. Step slightly in towards the horse with your outside foot so that your body moves towards him as you give him the signal with the wand, but do not position yourself right in front of him in case he walks on top of you. If you have fallen back by his shoulder you will not be able to do this.

● If he is really strong, turn the wand around so it is shorter and you can use the button on the end of the handle to tap him on the shoulder. You can also use the button end to gently tap his feet while in halt to improve awareness if he has a tendency to trip or stumble when working over poles.

● The wand is also used to indicate forward movement and/or the direction you want to go in by moving it from a point approximately two and a half feet (about 40cm) in front of his muzzle to around three feet (90cm) away.

● If your horse tries to hug too closely by your side, gently wave the whip between you both, or even touch him lightly with it on his neck, and step away to the side to keep your distance – *see* also the Homing Pigeon exercise.

LEADROPE, HANGING BACK AGAINST
See Tying up

LYING DOWN, FOR EXCESSIVE PERIODS
If a horse appears to be spending excessively long periods lying down, check for health issues such as laminitis, arthritis or colic. Most horses will scramble to their feet when a human approaches, although some may be confident and relaxed enough about your presence and their environment to remain down. However, a horse should be happy to get up if you slip a headcollar on and signal gently on the leadrope – though keep clear of his front feet as he does so. If he shows reluctance or is unable to do so it is likely that he is suffering some kind of physical problem.

LYING DOWN, RELUCTANCE TO
Horses generally take power naps of around 15 minutes rather than in long stretches, and thanks to the design of their legs are able to do this while standing up. As well as the slow-wave sleep experienced during these periods of dozing, they also need to experience REM (rapid eye movement) sleep, which only occurs while lying on their sides. This is a vulnerable position for a horse, so those which are kept on their own without another horse to act as lookout, or in an environment where they feel too stressed or insecure to lie down – or if they suffer from a physical condition which makes lying down and getting up again painful or have insufficient bedding – may suffer from sleep deprivation as a result. It is thought that REM sleep is linked to memory consolidation, so lack of it may lead to learning or memory problems.

The minimum amount of REM sleep needed may be as little as an hour spread over the space of several days, but it is necessary, so make every effort to provide a stress-free environment. Stabled horses generally sleep more at night when it is quieter, and you can generally tell from flattened areas of bedding whether they have been lying down, even if you don't actually see them.

LYING DOWN, WHILE RIDDEN
See Rolling

MAREISH BEHAVIOUR
All mares vary in their behaviour when in season: with some there is little difference, but others may become unpredictable in their response, less free moving, nappy, more sensitive around the flanks, irritable and even aggressive and liable to kick out while being handled and ridden. Behaviour can also vary between each season, as well as according to each stage of it, and some mares will be particularly difficult during the first and last season of the year; it may also become more apparent with age. Don't be too quick to discount other sources of physical discomfort as being the cause of irritable behaviour, however.

It is not known whether mares experience discomfort in the same way as humans, but it is possible that it does occur during ovulation, and certainly a little extra tact and care will not be out of place; reprimanding hormonal behaviour will achieve nothing and may actively damage your relationship.

Although various options are available, including medications to suppress oestrus, and over-the-counter herbal and feed supplements, if you have a difficult mare first ask your vet to give her a full health check, and then discuss the best course of action to take.

MOUNTING
See also Balance, Dismounting, Standing still

A horse that fidgets when the rider wants to mount, moves away, cowkicks, nips, hunches his back or bucks usually does so because he is uncomfortable or anticipates pain, whether from the rider sticking a toe in his side, landing heavily in the saddle, an ill-fitting or slipping saddle, or back pain. Holding the reins so they are too tight or with one shorter than the other to prevent the horse from nipping or otherwise expressing or trying to avoid the discomfort is counter-productive as it is liable to unbalance him, making it even harder for him to stand still. Lack of muscular strength or unpleasant associations with being ridden may also lead to difficulties.

Wherever possible, always use a mounting block: even if you consider yourself to be fairly athletic, mounting from the ground still imposes strain on both the horse's back and the saddle. If anyone is available, ask them to support the off-side stirrup, and reach across to the far side of the waist of the saddle to minimize sideways drag, which will unbalance and could cause injury to your horse.

If the horse has a tendency to walk off as you mount, it is far safer to mount facing forwards so that your foot is more parallel to the horse because you are then facing in the direction of travel. It also avoids excessive pulling on the saddle.

Mounting can cause concern to a youngster, and it is helpful to get him used to walking past someone standing on a mounting block and under a wand: this will help reduce his anxiety about movement above him. Work to make him more confident about movement around his sides and to improve his balance will also be beneficial. Where moving away from the rider has become an established habit, once the reason(s) for it has been resolved, he can be taught to stand quietly using clicker training.

Suggested exercises: Body Wraps, Clicker Targeting, Promise Wrap, Sliding Numnahs, Walking under Wands

MOUTHING
See Chewing

EXERCISE: STROKING THE LINE

This exercise can be useful in connection with a number of other issues as well as napping, including spooking, rearing, catching and bridling, and if the horse works above the vertical; it will also help to improve balance, hind-limb engagement, and the lengthening and strengthening of the topline.

The position of the horse's head will influence how he functions through the rest of his body. When the head is high, the flight/fight reflex is activated and the horse will tend to spin round when he is alarmed, rather than calmly turning his neck and head to look at something that may be causing him concern. Working from the ground, teaching the horse to lower his head – as opposed to simply dropping his head and neck on cue – will simultaneously release tension in his topline and is an invaluable exercise that will have far-reaching benefits. Lowering the head helps the horse to connect through the body, it reduces sensitivity in the back, improves balance and enables the horse to move beyond his instinctive responses.

It will also enable you to start the steps for correcting poor balance and crookedness through the neck, as you may notice that such a horse tends to stand with more weight through one forelimb than the other – most commonly horses weight their near foreleg with the neck and head positioned to the left. This is seen in all quadrupeds and is exacerbated by our own habitual handling of the horse.

There are different ways of teaching a horse to lower his head. Showing him how to release the bracing muscles in

Clip the leadrope to the side of the headcollar, and stroke the line from the top down. You only need to cover a short length, and remember to move your body at the same time. Avoid pulling the head down, as the aim is to teach the horse to soften into the contact.

his head and neck will quickly enable him to achieve a more desirable posture, whereas forcing the head down or training him to stand with a low head carriage will create bracing through the top and base of the neck.

If your horse finds it hard to stand still, it will be easiest to teach this exercise in the stable.

1. Stand on the near side with a soft leadline either attached to the headcollar as shown in the section 'Leading issues', or clipped to the side of the headcollar noseband.

2. Start slowly and reasonably firmly stroking down along the leadline, alternating between your right and left hand. Cover approximately eight inches (20cm) of the line with each stroke, and start as close to the headcollar as possible. Maintain a contact on the leadline at all times, so that you are constantly drawing it down, but without pulling. Pay attention to your posture and keep as relaxed as possible through your body. If you are standing in neutral pelvis you will achieve better results. If your horse is concerned, try looking down at the ground and keeping your own body low, as this can be less threatening than if you are standing braced and upright whilst looking up into the horse's eye. Do the exercise from both sides to avoid increasing any bias to one particular rein.

3. You can also try stroking the leadline with the left hand while your right hand rests gently on the top of the neck near the poll. Do small circular TTouches (*see* Chapter 5) on the opposite side of the neck with your fingertips, or do a gentle 'squeeze and release' on the top of the neck with your fingers and thumb.

If the horse is really braced against you, place one hand at the top of the neck as you stroke down the line, and gently rock his neck with your hand.

NAPPINESS

See also Mareish behaviour, Rearing, Separation anxiety

Being nappy is a common difficulty which usually occurs while hacking out, but it can also happen when working at home, typically when the horse is asked to move away from the entrance/exit of the work area. Young horses often have a 'green lean' towards the walls of working areas, but this is usually due to lack of strength and balance, rather than to nappiness.

A horse which is napping may begin to slow and then stop, or may come to a sudden and abrupt standstill without warning. He remains rooted to the spot refusing to move forwards, with forelegs braced and ignoring the leg aids; the headcarriage may become higher, and he will drop behind the bit. If the rider insists that he move forwards he will show resistance, laying his ears back, swishing his tail, humping his back, cowkicking, threatening to buck or rear, and/or running backwards. Hitting him, using more aggressive leg aids or shouting at him are likely only to succeed in increasing stress levels still further. If the opportunity arises, he may swing round abruptly, often dropping a shoulder as he does so, which can take the rider by surprise and be very unseating.

Napping can be related to separation anxiety, especially in the young inexperienced horse, or if they are anxious about something ahead, but it can also be due to physical discomfort caused by health issues, saddlery or the rider, to fatigue, weakness, lack of confidence, or if the horse is bored, or the work demanded is too excessive or difficult. When riding out, avoid taking linear routes where possible, as turning back on your tracks to return towards home can lead the horse to anticipate and try to turn early. When you do turn for home, it will invariably also be at a much faster speed than you want.

If your horse naps while riding out with another horse, the immediate solution is obvious: let the companion take the lead. Yours will usually take confidence from him (or be reluctant to be left behind) and will follow on. If on your own, it may be possible to dismount and lead him forwards, although watch your feet as he may not move straight and may crowd you if lacking in confidence. Bear in mind that you will need to remount at some point which may be difficult if the horse has become very wound up. You should also take care if you decide to turn round and retrace your footsteps, because the moment you do so, the horse may try to rush forwards and may become out of control.

Sometimes just stopping and waiting, and giving the horse a chance to assess things, can work. If his posture is very rooted, creating a little sideways movement can help: if you are leading, try wither rocking, or if riding, move both hands first to one side and then the other, while at the same time turning your shoulders in the same direction – but keep the movement slow and gentle so as not to encourage the horse to spin round and rush off at speed.

Whilst safety is important, try to avoid the temptation to gather up the reins, as this will increase tension in the horse's neck. Try Crest Releases to encourage him to soften his neck, if it is safe to do so, and remember to breathe. The mane at the wither will generally fall to the lower shoulder and this is usually the side that the horse will spin to, so be prepared and use a Balance Rein to support him through his lower shoulder if he habitually drops a shoulder to run for home.

In the long term you will obviously need to address those issues which underlie the difficulty, eliminating any sources of pain and developing confidence in working independently. If the horse's problem is fear-related or due to lack of experience, many of the TTEAM exercises outlined in this book will help cultivate his trust and self-assurance so that when asked to tackle something outside his range of experience, the horse will be prepared to trust your judgement. Particular exercises that may be of help are suggested below, but these aren't the only ones to try, just a place to start.

A horse which is known to nap can be dangerous to ride out on roads alone, so don't attempt to do so until you have resolved the problem. When testing it out, do so initially on off-road riding, and when first taking to the roads again go out with someone on foot or a bicycle in case you need help.

Suggested exercises: Body Wraps, Caterpillar, Ear Work, Forelock Pulls, Mouth Work, Neutral Pelvis, Rotating the Pelvis, Stroking the Line, Tail Work, Walking over Plastic, Walking up Behind, Wand Work, Wither Rocking

NIPPING
See Aggression, Bullying

ON THE FOREHAND
See Balance, on the forehand

OTHER ANIMALS, FEAR OF
See also Balance, Bolting, Bucking, Clumsiness, Leading issues, Outline, Saddling issues, Spooking, Standing still

Horses may fear other species for many reasons – they may have been chased by a dog, for example, or it may be due to the unpredictability of the movement, the smell, the noise or the different shape of that animal.

As with all behavioural problems there are often associated issues such as a general lack of confidence or high levels of stress, so ground work and body work aimed at reducing tension in the body and improving self-confidence and self-control will go a long way to reducing anxiety all round.

Clicker training is another excellent tool when working with a horse that has a fear of anything, provided the steps are small and relatively easy to achieve. Ignore those who tell you not to use a clicker with a fearful animal: it is not possible to re-create an emotion with the clicker, and far from reinforcing the fear, it can help to change a negative association into a more positive one. It helps the horse to think, and to focus on something other than the object of concern.

You may need to be creative in the way you work to resolve or at least diminish this problem, but it can be useful to break it down into small steps. For example, playing a sound recording of that animal on a low level while the horse is engaged in something pleasant such as eating, or doing some clicker games, can be a useful starting point, and you can gradually increase the volume over several sessions so that the horse becomes accustomed to the noise without being exposed to the visual and olfactory stimuli all at once. Remember that his hearing is more acute than yours. You can also experiment with cut-out shapes of different animals attached to jump fillers and incorporate them into the ground-work exercises before riding past them in an arena.

When out, use a Balance Rein so that you don't shorten the reins in response to his fear, and use the Rotating the Pelvis exercise (*see* problem 'Rushing, while ridden') to encourage him to move forwards if he braces and goes into freeze. A Promise Wrap (*see* problem 'Standing still, halting while ridden') can also help with general levels of confidence and spatial awareness, and can be another useful tool in helping him move beyond his instinctive responses.

Suggested exercises: Body Wraps, Clicker Targeting, Mouth Work, Stroking the Line, Tail Work, Wand Work

OUTLINE
See also Balance, Bit evasions, Crookedness, Over-excitable, Pulling, Rushing, Spookiness

If a horse struggles to produce a correct outline, it is important to look for the reasons why: conformation can make it difficult for some, and you may need to find a compromise between the classical dressage ideal and what your horse can realistically and comfortably achieve. Other areas of investigation include incorrectly developed musculature, dental problems, bitting, saddle fit, weakness, fatigue, lack of balance, poor proprioceptive sense, spookiness, shoeing and foot balance. Furthermore, don't forget your own influence: everything you do while in the saddle affects the horse in some way for better or worse, yet we often put ourselves down last on the list of 'things to check'.

When considering outline, it is important to remember that this refers to the whole of the horse's body, and not just to the position of his head and neck. However, if you have acquired

EXERCISE: FORELOCK PULLS

Sarah developed this exercise as an adaptation of the TTEAM Tail Work for a horse that was suspicious of contact around the hindquarters; it is an excellent addition to other exercises aimed at releasing and lengthening the horse's neck, and also helps to create movement through the whole topline. It can be done as part of a body-work routine, or prior to or during ridden work. It is especially good for horses that find it hard to work on a free rein, and can also be helpful with horses which dislike being caught, and those which are ear shy. Teach Forelock Circles and Slides (*see* problem 'Bridle, difficult to') before trying this exercise.

Support the horse's head by resting one hand on the noseband, and take the forelock in the other hand. Stand with one foot back and transfer your weight from the front foot to the other foot. As you move the horse should move with you. Hold the position for a moment and then slowly transfer your weight forwards. You should see the chest muscles moving, and ideally the movement should continue through the length of the back, but if your horse is tight the movement will be minimal initially.

1. Stand in front of and slightly to one side of your horse. Rest one hand lightly on the headcollar or bridle browband, keeping your fingers open and taking care not to tighten your grip. Place one foot further forward than the other.
2. Gently take the forelock and stroke the hair lightly from the base right out to the end. If your horse is happy for you to do this, take the forelock by the base again, and this time keep hold of it. Gently rocking your weight on to your back foot, draw your horse's neck towards you.
3. Hold for a moment, and then slowly transfer your weight on to your front foot, guiding the movement back to where it started. This release of tension on the forelock needs to be the longest part of the exercise. Watch the withers, chest muscles, shoulders and back whilst you are working. You should see movement through the entire body although some horses may be so blocked to begin with that the movement is minimal or restricted to certain parts of their body.

EXERCISE: MEET AND MELT

When a horse pulls or leans on the bit, the natural inclination is to pull back, or to try and get him off the bit with a quick correction. A more effective way is to gently meet the pressure he is applying to the bit with an equal amount of pressure on the reins, and then to soften that pressure by slowly

If the horse leans on the bit, meet the pressure without pulling on his mouth.

'melting' through your hands and body. As you melt, give a long, slow exhalation of breath as if you were blowing out a candle: this will help you soften through your sternum, shoulders and arms. This exercise, as with others, will be most effective if you are riding in neutral pelvis, as it may be your own posture that is contributing to the horse's problems by pushing him on to the forehand.

As you slowly release, the horse will often offer the same response, which encourages him to soften through his jaw and neck and teaches him self-carriage. This is also useful for horses that tend to brace through one side of the body or work above the vertical. Avoid throwing away the contact, as this will only exacerbate the horse's imbalance, and slightly rotate your body slowly to the left and right as you meet and melt if your horse is moving forwards with a braced body and back. Be careful also that you do not grip upwards or swing the lower legs back as you do this exercise.

Slowly 'melt' the contact by taking your arms forward if necessary: this encourages the horse to soften in the mouth and neck. Once he has learned to 'melt' into the contact your own movements can be more subtle. Avoid throwing the rein away, and melt slowly so that he feels the contact and does not fall further on to the forehand.

EXERCISE: NECK ROCKING

This is a really simple exercise which helps relax tight ligaments and muscles and releases tension through the withers, shoulders, back, poll and jaw.

1. The exercise can be done from either side, but assuming you are standing on the horse's near side, stand with your feet spaced comfortably apart and with your hip and knee joints slightly flexed. Place the palm of your right hand on top of the crest, and the palm of your left hand underneath the neck. Keep both hands in line with each other, allowing your fingers to gently cup the top and bottom of the neck without gripping.
2. Bring the crest slightly towards you with your right hand, whilst simultaneously moving the bottom of the neck slightly away from you with the left hand.
3. Then guide the crest away from you with the right hand as your left hand draws the bottom of the neck towards you.
4. This exercise is done quite quickly, so you are in fact jiggling or rocking the neck. You can start it at any point on the neck – if you can work all the way from poll to withers or withers to poll, so much the better; however, some horses are so tight in the neck they can only tolerate contact in certain places initially. In such cases, after a few neck rocks in an 'acceptable' area, the neck often releases enough to allow you to work the whole of it.

Place your hands on the top and bottom of the horse's neck, and bring one hand towards you as the other hand moves away. Vary the speed with which you make this rocking movement, and start at the base of the neck. Watch the horse's responses, and work up the neck if appropriate.

EXERCISE: CREST RELEASE

This exercise can be done while riding, and will encourage the horse to lower and lengthen his neck, helping those that find it hard to release into a soft rein contact.

1. Start doing the exercise whilst the horse is standing still. Hold the reins in one hand and place the other on top of the horse's neck, palm down, with fingers and thumb on either side of the crest.
2. Push your hand up the crest from the base of the neck towards the head, only moving it as far as you can go safely and comfortably. Make sure that you don't allow your lower leg to slide backwards on the horse's sides. You should begin to notice a difference in posture after just a few repetitions.

If the horse is in the habit of flinging his head up, start by working only on the lower part of the neck to avoid getting hit in the face.

Take the reins in one hand and run your other hand up the horse's crest to encourage him to release and lengthen his neck. Ensure that your lower leg does not slide backwards as you move your upper body forwards.

a horse which habitually moves with a high headcarriage or in an overbent posture you may have to focus a little extra attention on this part of his body. Although not the sole cause, very often tension in the neck contributes to both these problems and will affect not only the quality of your rein contact and overall outline, but your horse's ability to learn.

Neck tension may also influence the optic nerve, causing problems with spatial awareness, depth perception and changes in light, which can make it hard for horses moving in and out of trailers, boxes and stables. They may also be spooky and exhibit concern about bright objects – this may be worse in summer when more light is reflected off shiny surfaces such as white boards, cars and water.

The following four exercises will be beneficial with both high-headed and overbent postures. Even if you don't feel you have any major problems, they are still worth trying, and you may find yourself pleasantly surprised at how much they help improve the horse's whole way of going.

Suggested exercises: Balance Rein, Caterpillar, Crest Release, Ear Work, Floating Forwards, Forelock Pulls, Jowl Release, Meet and Melt, Mouth Work, Neck Rocking, Neutral Pelvis, Rotating the Pelvis, Sternum Lifts, Stroking the Line, Tail Work

OVERBENDING
See Outline

OVER-EXCITABLE
See also Balance, Jogging, Rushing

New situations, the atmosphere at a show, or anticipation of work such as a gallop or jumping can cause horses to become over-excited, inattentive to the handler or rider, and more difficult to control as a result. Often, however, this 'excitement' is misunderstood and is not in fact expressing pleasure, as we tend to think, but rather is a behaviour linked to being stressed.

Diet and over-confinement with insufficient time out at grass, insufficient forage when he is stabled, plus the horse's innate temperament, can all contribute to his tendency to become excitable. It is also important to be sure that behaviour that we take for expressing excitement is not in fact expressing symptoms of pain; also that a narrow fitting saddle is not pushing the horse's back down, which will

---

EXERCISE: DEEP BREATHING

Breathing correctly and regularly can have a massive effect on your posture: you will quickly notice the benefits, not just in the way the horse goes, but in your ability to sit more softly and closely in trot and canter.

1. Start by practising this sitting on a chair so there are no distractions. Choose a chair with a firm, level seat and find the neutral pelvis position (*see* problem 'Canter, changing leads').
2. Place the palm of one hand on your abdomen, just above your navel. Breathe in deeply through your nose for a count of ten, allowing it to move your hand out.
3. Hold your breath for a count of five, using your diaphragm to help hold the air in – don't press your lips tightly together but keep them very slightly parted.
4. Release your breath slowly between your lips over a count of ten.
5. Once you have gained a feel for the exercise try it while mounted, though keep both hands on the reins. It can also be a useful exercise to use before riding to help eliminate any tension.

automatically raise his head, thereby increasing his predisposition to flight.

Much can be done to help reduce the horse's reactive tendency, through adopting a management and training philosophy that is better suited to the horse (*see* Part 2) as well as by using TTEAM bodywork (*see* Chapter 5) to help reduce stress levels. Introduce new work in small, easy steps, and bear in mind that when riding and handling any horse you need to be relaxed both mentally and physically; in particular, when engaging in activities more likely to excite your horse, try to be especially aware of your breathing – or lack of it. If you are nervous yourself, excited or concentrating hard on accomplishing some work with the horse, it is likely that you will either hold your breath or begin to take more rapid and shallower breaths. This will create tension within you, which in turn will affect your posture, and this, combined with your breathing, will be interpreted by the horse as an indication of concern, and he will start to prepare himself for flight.

Make a point of checking how you are breathing, particularly if you feel the horse starting to become tense. Always think in terms of breathing out – breathing in will take care of itself! Don't let your breath whoosh out if you find you have been holding it, but let it escape slowly, and completely. This moment of releasing your breath will simultaneously release tension in you, which the horse will respond to.

Suggested exercises: Balance Rein, Body Wraps, Crest Release, Deep Breathing, Forelock Pulls, Promise Wrap, Rotating the Pelvis, Stroking the Line, Tail Work

PAWING
See also Balance, Bedding, digging up, Halting, Rolling, Standing still

Pawing is usually behaviour that stems from frustration, and can be seen in a horse that has a strong desire to move forward but is being prevented from doing so, whether by a handler, a rider or a stable door; it can also be seen in horses that find it hard to stand in balance due to poor posture. Over-confinement, insufficient exercise and turnout, and poor balance will predispose to this behaviour. It frequently happens at feed times, again generally due to impatience and frustration at the food not arriving quickly enough.

Pawing can also be a way of investigating the ground – be careful if your horse starts to paw at the ground or if standing in water while you are riding as it is often a preliminary to rolling. It is also a behaviour associated with colic.

PICA
See also Chewing, Coprophagia

Ranging from licking to actually ingesting non-food substances such as sand, soil, wood, twigs, bark, faeces and urine, this behaviour may be due to an underlying health problem, hunger, dietary deficiency, and/or boredom. It can also become an established habit which continues after the initial cause is remedied. As well as addressing health and feeding issues with the assistance of your vet and an equine nutritionist, ensure adequate turn-out time and provide a more stimulating stable environment; also consider increasing exercise if appropriate.

Suggested exercises: Belly Lifts, Ear Work, Lick of the Cow's Tongue, Mouth Work

PIGS, FEAR OF
See Other animals, fear of

PULLING, WHILE LED
See Leading

PULLING, WHILE RIDDEN
See also Balance, Bolting, Leading, Outline, Over-excitable, Snatching at the reins, Standing still

EXERCISE: STROKING THE REINS

This Connected Riding exercise helps your horse release through the jaw, poll, neck and back if he is bracing and leaning on the bit. It is also beneficial for horses which lean on one rein, rush, spook or spin round.

1. Ask someone to hold your horse on a leadline while doing this exercise. Start off trying it in halt first, and then in walk.

Stroke the reins by taking the reins in one hand and passing your other hand over the top to pick up the reins.

2. Stroke along the reins, sliding each hand in turn from just behind the horse's neck to a point just in front of your body. As one hand begins moving towards you, place the other just ahead of it and begin the next stroking movement so that it becomes a soft, rhythmical flow of movement.

Repeat the movement so that you are constantly stroking along the reins to encourage the horse to soften in the jaw and neck.

3. Be careful not to inadvertently clamp your legs on whilst doing this exercise. Use plain leather reins without grips so your hands can slide freely along them.

Stroking one rein can help the horse to increase his stride length if he falls through one shoulder and leans on one rein.

4. If your horse tends to lean on one rein, try it as you ride through turns and circles.

You can also stroke one rein as you ask the horse to turn, to soften his neck. This exercise also prevents the rider from pulling back with the hand, which will cause the horse to brace himself through the jaw and neck.

Approximately 60 per cent of the horse's bodyweight is naturally carried over the forelimbs, so a high proportion of horses work on the forehand as a result. Conformation or growth spurts where the horse is croup high will also create bracing around the back of the shoulders, which can cause the horse to lean on the bit or pull. Other contributory factors include fatigue, restricted movement through the back, and an inability to engage the powerful muscles of the hindquarters for propulsion. The rider may also inadvertently play a part in the problem through driving the horse on to the forehand with the seat bones, leaning forward, taking a heavy rein contact, carrying the hands too low, or from asking the horse to consistently work in an overbent outline with his face behind the vertical so that the neck, which is used for balance, develops incorrectly.

Dental problems can be another area to check, also the fit of saddle, bridle and bit – it is important to ensure they are not inhibiting the correct movement of the horse in any way.

Improving core strength and hind-limb engagement will enable the horse to balance more effectively without leaning on the bit for support. The use of frequent half halts and transitions can assist in this, but avoid making sharp corrections with the bit which can bruise the tongue and bars and will do little to teach the horse how to work in a more elevated frame. The exercises Balance Rein (*see* problem 'Balance, on the Forehand') and Sternum Lifts (*see* problem 'Balance, lack of Physical') are invaluable in teaching your horse how to move his centre of gravity backwards; try also using Body Wraps (*see* Chapter 5, section 'Equipment') and ground-work exercises over and around different patterns of poles to improve the horse's self-carriage and proprioceptive sense.

It takes two to pull, so don't forget to include yourself: changing your own habitual response is essential to breaking this cycle. The Connected Riding exercises Rotating the Pelvis (*see* problem 'Rushing while Ridden'), Floating Forwards (*see* problem 'Canter, disunited') and Meet and Melt (*see* problem 'Outline') will all help to prevent you from bracing and pulling back, which often exacerbates the problem; they will also enable you to maintain a correct hand position.

Suggested exercises: Labyrinth, Raised Polework, Solo Polework, Stroking the Line, Stroking the Reins, ZigZag

PULLING, MANE AND TAIL
See Trimming, Clipping

QUIDDING
See Eating

REARING
See also Bolting, Bucking, Nappiness, Separation anxiety

Rearing is potentially very dangerous for both horse and rider and may occur if the horse naps (see problem 'Nappiness') and the rider tries to force the horse forwards; it is also often associated with dental issues such as wolf teeth (full, broken and blind), hooks on molars, bruised bars and/or a sore tongue. Fear, excessively strong rein aids which restrict forward movement, especially if combined with forceful or punishing leg aids, pain in the forelimbs, and tension in the upper part of the neck can also be contributory factors.

As with the majority of unwanted behaviours, it is likely that there is a pattern. The horse may have held his breath when he was first girthed up, and then rears when you ask him to move off or after a few strides; or he may rear when you ask him to leave the yard, or turn him away from his friends when out hacking; or he may be afraid of passing something that spooked him on a previous ride or in the school. This behaviour is common in youngsters that have had a fright. Regardless of how long the behaviour has been established, it is an indicator that the horse feels unsafe – as is true of most unwanted behaviours.

Some horses that rear may have unlevel ears, indicating changes in the first two cervical vertebrae in the neck; but even if you can't spot anything untoward, ask your vet to examine him so that you can rule out physical pain as a cause, and to refer you to an equine physiotherapist.

You will also need to check that your tack fits correctly, as an ill-fitting saddle can cause the horse to dip his back and raise his neck, thereby inhibiting his ability to move forwards from the leg and increasing the likelihood of rearing. Tension round the back of the shoulders can also cause problems for the horse when he is girthed up, and even a mild bit can cause acute discomfort if it is the wrong size for his mouth or fitted incorrectly, while pressure across the poll from a browband that is too narrow or a headstall that is too tight can also exacerbate this problem.

If your horse does start to rear, keep the rein contact slack and try to keep your body leaning forwards so you remain in balance and minimize the risk of him losing his footing and falling – put your arms round his neck to help you if necessary. If he does more than just lifting his front feet a little way off the ground, slip both feet out of the stirrups and slide off to one side rather than risk him falling, possibly with you beneath him. Hitting him under the belly with a long rope, smashing eggs on his poll and similar techniques are aggressive actions and unlikely to help. Pulling him over to teach him a lesson is also dangerous and inhumane.

If your horse rears in hand ensure that you always wear a hat and gloves and buy a long leadline so that you can let the line run through your hand and step away to the side if he goes up. Make sure that it does not have a heavy clip, as weight on the line may be a contributory factor if he is sore in the upper part of his neck. Don't attempt to pull him down as

pressure on the poll will probably trigger him to rear again. As well as the exercises suggested below, work on the ground over patterns of poles to improve his co-ordination, self-confidence and self control will all be beneficial.

Suggested exercises: Balance Rein, Body Wraps, Ear Work, Forelock Pulls, Labyrinth, Stroking the Line, Labyrinth, ZigZag

ROLLING
See also Rug tearing

Horses roll to relieve itchiness, to help get rid of loose coat hairs when shedding their winter coat, if they are hot and sweaty, and to cover themselves with an insulating layer of mud during cold weather. Colic, sweet itch or parasitic infestations and irritating skin conditions can also be the cause of vigorous rolling. Sometimes the urge to roll is so strong that the horse will attempt to do so while the rider is on board, most often when standing in water or on soft ground such as sand or the artificial surface of a school – although in the case of colic it may occur anywhere.

The first indication that a horse is going to roll is that he lowers his head and sniffs or snorts gently at the ground, and paws with a front foot; then his front legs will buckle at the knees as he starts to go down. If you can keep his head up and move him forwards you may be able to prevent him going down, though once his knees touch the floor it is usually too late.

If you are mounted, quickly take your feet out of the stirrups and dismount on the side to which the horse is dropping his shoulder so you keep away from his hooves. You may still at this point be able to stop him from rolling if you can keep his head up and urge him to his feet again. Should your horse succeed in rolling on his saddle, have both it and his back checked for possible damage. If colic is suspected, call your vet immediately, as this is a medical emergency and the horse may be in severe pain.

If it is safe to do so, Ear Work (*see* problem 'Catching, Difficulty in') while waiting for the vet to arrive may be of help. Check the saddle fit, too, as horses that are irritated by an unbalanced rider and/or an ill-fitting saddle may roll to relieve themselves of the source of discomfort.

RUBBING, MANE AND/OR TAIL
See also Travelling, Trimming up

A horse will usually rub his mane and tail because of some kind of irritation – it may be a skin disease, parasites or an allergic reaction. Ask your vet to examine him to diagnose the problem so it can be correctly treated.

Rubbing may also occur if the horse is sore from having had his mane pulled, particularly if too much hair was taken out in one session, or from itchiness if shampoo suds were not washed out thoroughly after bathing. Always use bathing products designed specifically for horses, as those intended for humans, dirty dishes or laundry can sometimes cause irritation.

If the tail is rubbed during travelling, it may be because the horse is leaning on it against the partition or ramp behind him for balance. Protecting it with a bandage and tail guard will help prevent further damage, but you should also look into ways of improving your horse's balance while in transit, and should check on your own driving if you want him to continue to be easy to load and transport.

Tail hairs may be damaged if the horse is suffering some kind of discomfort and is resting his quarters against a fixed manger or partition in his stable in an attempt to relieve it – laminitis or pain in the lumbar region are typical examples of this.

RUBBING, RIDER AGAINST OBJECTS
See also Balance, Crookedness, Doors, Rolling
Although it is not unheard of for a horse to deliberately attempt to rub his rider off against a fixed object such as fencing, school walls, gate posts and trees, it is rare, and it may actually be that he is trying to relieve itchiness: some conditions such as sweet itch can produce an irresistible urge to scratch vigorously against anything available, even though a rider may be on board at the time. In the absence of anything else available, some will drop to the ground and roll in an effort to relieve the discomfort.

Passing too close to objects may also be due to a horse having poor spatial awareness and proprioceptive sense – but even where this is good, remember that the horse won't make allowance for a rider's legs hanging down his sides. Therefore open gates wide enough to allow plenty of room to pass through, and take special care if the ground is muddy or a puddle has formed in the centre of it, because the horse may try to step round the side of it.

Where a horse shows a tendency to hug the school walls rather too close for comfort, the problem may be related to lack of balance and straightness. Riders can also be responsible for exacerbating or even creating the problem if the way they apply the aids is unbalanced and incorrect: too much inside leg and inside rein, unsupported by the outside leg and rein, will lead to the horse creeping ever closer towards the wall. Time spent working on the inside track will help to teach the horse greater psychological and physical independence of the walls, and will improve his balance and straightness, while practising exercises such as leg yielding towards the centre line and counter flexion can help the rider become more aware of the effects of the aids, and to apply them more appropriately.

Suggested exercises: Balance Rein, Body Wraps, Leg Circles, Narrow Spaces Exercise, Rotating the Pelvis, Sliding Numnahs, Walking over Plastic, Wand Work

RUGS, TEARING
See also Aggression, Bullying, Stereotypies

An ill-fitting rug, a rug that slips, and/or a dirty lining can cause discomfort, and not surprisingly lead to the horse trying to remove the source of it. Sometimes linings may be clean, but either the fabric itself may cause irritation, or the type of detergent used to wash the rug. Overheating can be another cause of rug tearing: modern thermal fabrics work very efficiently and many people over-rug – slide a hand beneath it to check that your horse doesn't feel uncomfortably warm. Boredom may be another point to consider: in winter when most horses will be wearing rugs, they may be spending longer periods stabled, and when turned out there may be little grazing available.

It may not necessarily be the rug that is to blame; a horse suffering from an itchy skin condition or parasites may simply be trying to relieve the irritation by scratching with his teeth or by rubbing his body against trees, gateposts and other objects, and the rug simply gets in the way. Sometimes it is a grazing companion that is doing the damage: using taste deterrents sometimes helps, although more often their effectiveness is limited and it may be necessary to turn an established rug tearer out in another paddock either by himself or with horses which do not need rugging up.

A horse which is not accustomed to wearing a rug may take exception to it and do his best to remove it, so spend as much time carefully preparing a youngster for this as you would introducing a saddle, rather than expecting him to calmly put up with something of which he has had no previous experience.

Suggested exercises: Body Wraps, Sliding Numnahs, Wand Work

RUSHING, WHILE LED
See Leading issues

RUSHING, WHILE RIDDEN
See also Balance, Bolting, Jogging, Jumping, running out, Leading issues, Over-excitement, Spooking

Rushing is rarely a sign of enthusiasm, and is more likely to be due to discomfort and/or anxiety – a case of wanting to get something over and done with as quickly as possible – and/or to lack of balance and poor co-ordination. It's important not to reprimand a horse for it, as this will only make the situation worse. Over-sensitivity to leg aids can also be a contributory cause, and teaching exercises such

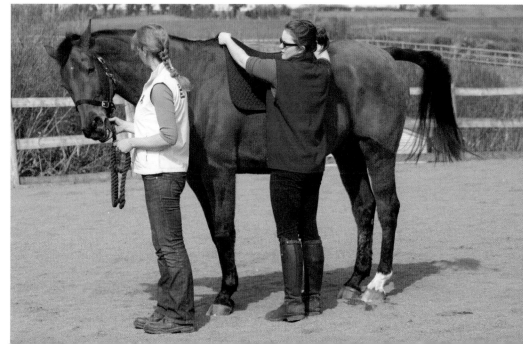

If the horse has saddling issues his body language will change when you approach him with a numnah, or if he hears the stirrups or girth buckles clinking as you walk towards him with the saddle. Note the swishing of the tail and the open mouth in this picture.

EXERCISE: ROTATING THE PELVIS

Learning to rotate your hips from the neutral pelvis position can really help the horse under saddle; it will also help you to alter several of your own habits, such as dropping a hip or a shoulder. This exercise will help to free the horse through his barrel and spine, will improve his balance and co-ordination, and enable him to release from the poll right through to the hindquarters. It forms part of the Connected Riding technique, and has an incredibly powerful effect on the horse as it will help him to lengthen and strengthen his topline and engage his hindquarters.

1. Find neutral pelvis (see problem 'Canter, changing leads'). Make a small, smooth, swivelling motion slowly from side to side. You need to ensure that you are rotating from the pelvis and not simply twisting through the upper body. If the motion comes from your pelvic girdle, your legs will move slightly as you swivel; if you are twisting from the upper body your legs will remain braced and you will pull unevenly on the horse's mouth because you will drop your shoulder as you turn. Done correctly, this exercise will give the horse a gentle 'meet and melt' sensation (*see* exercise in problem 'Outline') on both reins, which will encourage him to soften through the neck.

2. Swivel to the left to help the horse through a left turn, and swivel to the right to help him on a right bend. If he braces and rushes, whether working in the school or out on a hack, try alternate swivels to left and right as these can help to slow down a horse that might be rushing due to tension in his back. This will also unlock your back, which may be contributing to the problem.

TOP: *Find neutral pelvis, and then slowly swivel your body from your pelvis to the right. Make sure that you do not twist through the body or drop your right shoulder. Keep your leg contact soft round the horse's body so that you do not squeeze him between your calves, as this will restrict his movement through his ribs and back. The swivel movement should be subtle and not over-exaggerated.*

BOTTOM: *Swivel to the left to make a slight turn to the left, and alternate between rotating right and left to slow the horse when he starts to brace himself and rush.*

as Sliding Numnahs (*see* problem 'Door, rushing through'), Wand Work (*see* problem 'Grooming issues'), Body wraps (Chapter 5, 'Equipment') and various TTouches (*see* Chapter 5) can help to reduce levels of concern about his sides being touched.

Suggested exercises: Balance Rein, Lick of the Cow's Tongue, Mouth Work, Narrow Spaces Exercise, Promise Wrap, Rotating the Pelvis, Tail Work

SADDLING ISSUES
See also Cold-backed, Girthing issues, Mareish behaviour

Poor saddle fit is a common problem when there are saddling issues: the discomfort can trigger a host of unwanted behaviours, and many horses will express concern when saddled. They may move away, hunch their back, pin back their ears, cowkick, or attempt to bite or grab the leadrope – and sometimes these actions will start from the moment they *see* the saddle. The horse may be reluctant to let you mount, and may jog or be reluctant to move once you are on board. Any loss of muscle around the back of the shoulder, and rub marks on either side of the spine, particularly around the back of the saddle area, are usually indicative of poor saddle fit or placement. You may also notice that sweat and grease marks on the saddle cloth are uneven, which can be another indicator of a poorly fitting saddle – or of a crooked horse or rider, which in turn will cause a negative association with the saddle.

If you are experiencing problems, any discomfort in the back should be ruled out by a veterinary surgeon. It is also worth getting a couple of opinions as to what type of saddle will best suit your horse, as well as advice on fit.

Some horses have an expectation of discomfort due to previous problems, even after saddle fit and physical problems have been corrected. Be gentle when putting on and taking off the saddle: avoid dropping it heavily on the horse's back, and make sure the stirrup irons are run up and the girth is placed over the top of the saddle to avoid banging the horse's sides or spine. When lowering the girth, go round to the other side and take it quietly off the saddle, as throwing it over to the other side of the horse may result in it banging his legs. Try putting the saddle on from the off side to break the pattern, and read the section 'Girthing issues' for more tips to help both you and the horse. Bear in mind that if the horse is tense due to concerns about the saddle you will be starting with a problem even before you mount.

If working with a youngster, or if re-starting a horse, introduce the saddle in easy stages. The exercise Sliding Numnahs (*see* problem 'Door, rushing through') is excellent for any horse, as it gives him a new experience of having something on his back; also working him in hand with a numnah under a half wrap is another useful stepping stone.

Suggested exercises: Belly lifts, Body Wraps (Half Wrap), Ear Work, Lick of the Cow's Tongue, Tail Work

SEPARATION ANXIETY
See also Balance, lack of emotional, Nappiness

Some horses form very close bonds of attachment with other individuals, but lack of self-assurance, as well as lack of confidence in the handler and anxiety about what he is being asked to do, can also lead to a horse being reluctant to leave other horses. If insisted upon, he may comply, but not happily: he may call to his companions and be in a state of heightened alert with a high head carriage, shortened elevated steps, stiffly pricked ears and a high tail carriage, and he may feel hard and unresponsive to hand and leg aids. Some will eventually settle, but others remain anxious and may nap or attempt to spin round in an attempt to return to their friends.

Developing trust while continuing to promote the horse's own self-confidence is essential to solving the issue. Spending time working at home using TTEAM TTouches (*see* Chapter 5) and in-hand ground-work exercises can be the perfect way of achieving this; if the horse is very anxious about being on his own, do this work while another horse is present. As he begins to settle and relax, the other horse can be gradually moved further away.

Introduce ridden work, too, taking the opportunity to try exercises that will help increase his independence, such as riding alongside another horse, then taking the lead from it, dropping behind it, circling away and varying your distance from it. If the horse becomes concerned at any point, allow him to move a little closer to the other horse, and once he is relaxed again, ask him to move away once more.

You can introduce this in easy steps into your hacking, too, going out with a steady and sensible escort horse and taking it in turns to lead. Try gradually increasing the distance between you both, and when approaching home and you can ride with a distance of at least fifty feet between you, tell your escort to turn off so you can complete the last hundred yards or so on your own – when he is so close to home the horse may be less concerned by the disappearance of his hacking buddy, and be happy to head towards his stable without fuss. You can then gradually start to increase these distances.

If the horse has to be kept stabled for some reason and is isolated from other equine company, he may also show signs of stress, although this may take the form of stereotypies such as box walking or weaving. In this situation it may be worth installing a stable mirror to provide him with a form of companionship.

Suggested exercises: Body Wraps, Labyrinth, Mouth Work, Promise Wrap, Solo Polework

SHOEING, DIFFICULTY IN
See Feet, difficult to shoe

SHYING
See Spooking

SNATCHING AT THE REINS
See also Balance, Bit evasions, Headshaking, Jogging, Pulling, while ridden

Snatching at the reins is frequently due to discomfort, and while the mouth and bridle are obvious places to look for problems, this behaviour can be caused by pain anywhere in the rest of the body or limbs.

It can also happen if the horse is tired, or if he has been worked excessively in an outline, when he will seek the freedom to stretch and lower his head and neck. He may also open his mouth, yawing at the bit and shaking his head and neck as he does so, although not always.

Over-severe bitting, and an erratic or heavy and restrictive rein contact may also be responsible: it can be instructive to have a lunge lesson when you can work without reins, as this will help determine if you are relying on them to a certain extent to maintain your balance. Lunge lessons will also help you to improve your posture, and to learn how to be self-supporting.

Using a Balance Rein (*see* problem 'Balance, on the forehand') can also be a big help, particularly if you have a horse that tends to lean on the bit or go on the forehand, as it will help you rebalance him without feeling the need to support and balance him with a strong rein contact.

If the horse snatches when you offer him a free rein you will need to check the fit of the saddle, as a narrow tree which inhibits the ability to release and lengthen the topline is often to blame.

Suggested exercises: Crest Release, Forelock Pulls, Reverse Reins, Stroking the Reins, Tail Work

SPOOKING

See also Balance, lack of emotional, Clumsiness, Jogging, Nappiness, Outline

Spooking is a common problem with many horses, and one which can be very dangerous for both horse and human – and if riding out on the road, for other road users too. Spooky horses are easily startled, often noise sensitive, and as well as being wary of unfamiliar objects, may show concern about familiar things in unaccustomed places, or even the absence of something from its expected place. A horse's anxiety may cause him to adopt a shortened and elevated step and headcarriage with stiffly pricked ears, often accompanied by much snorting and blowing; he may jump sideways, and as with napping, may be reluctant to pass the object or place.

If urged on he will attempt to keep as far away from the object of anxiety as possible, will try to keep his head and shoulders positioned towards it so as to keep it in clear view, and may attempt to rush past or, if given the opportunity, will spin round and set off at speed in the opposite direction. It is worth checking your horse's vision and hearing, as these can sometimes be an underlying or contributory cause to spookiness.

Spooky behaviour is an indicator that your horse doesn't feel safe; however, it is possible to take steps to reduce your horse's concerns – if you don't, the behaviour may escalate. One school of thought recommends de-sensitizing the horse by constantly exposing him to the object of his fear – but we are not convinced by either the wisdom or the efficacy of this course. Unless extremely carefully and slowly managed, the repeated exposure may actually reinforce fears rather than reduce them: in addition, it is rarely just one object the horse is anxious about, but rather a whole variety. As it is impossible to introduce every single possible object in every possible location the horse is likely to meet, we find that other methods are more successful. In addition, desensitization can also be difficult to manage safely, and may put you and your horse in a potentially dangerous situation.

Using TTouch body work (*see* Chapter 5) on a regular daily basis can be extremely helpful: it won't necessarily stop your horse from spooking, but because it can help to release tension and change his posture, it can make such episodes less frequent and less dramatic, and your horse will calm down more quickly after each episode.

Body work is also a good way of helping to form a bond of trust and confidence between you, so that your horse will be more inclined to pass something scary if you ask him to. Body work can also be a good way of helping to de-stress yourself: if you are expecting the horse to be spooky, the anticipatory tension in your own body will be apparent to him, and may cause him to be in an even higher state of alert.

Although it can be tempting to ride the horse in an over-exaggerated outline in an attempt to give yourself a feeling of extra control, constantly asking for an overbent posture with the face behind the vertical creates a lot of tension in the neck and inhibits free forward movement. Typically, spooky horses also have a tight tail, which feels clamped instead of relaxed when you try to lift it, so these can both be key areas to work on – include neck and tail work at any point during your daily routine, and do some before work, too. Wand Work (*see* problem Grooming issues') can also be beneficial, as spooky horses often have poor spatial awareness, and stroking all over the body and limbs will help to calm and relax them while at the same time creating better self-awareness, proprioceptive sense, and integration of mind and body. TTEAM ground-work exercises should also be taught, as these can be instrumental in helping to develop confidence and the ability to cope in unknown or worrying situations.

Using a Balance Rein (*see* Balance, on the forehand) while riding will also be helpful: and

EXERCISE: CATERPILLAR

Tension in the neck affects spatial awareness, the ability to learn, and can cause problems with depth perception and changes in light. This can make it hard for horses when moving into or out of trailers, boxes and stables, and they may be inclined to be spooky, and to exhibit concern about bright objects. Pushy behaviour or crowding when being handled can also often be attributed to tension in some part of the neck.

Signs of tension in the neck include incorrect muscling, with over-bulking and under-development of the appropriate muscles, a tight or non-existent topline, over-defined cervical vertebrae, and you may notice the mane 'jumping' as your horse lowers or raises his head. Changes in the way the mane lies often correspond to areas where tension is present.

This is a Connected Riding exercise that can be done while the horse is standing still or on the move. It helps reduce soft tissue tension around the cervical vertebrae, enabling him to lengthen and release through his neck, and helping him to establish true self-carriage.

1. Stand on the left side of the horse, and support the head either by lightly hooking your fingers on to the bridle or headcollar noseband, or by holding the leadline close to the headcollar with your right hand.
2. Place your left hand on the base of your horse's neck just above the point of the shoulder. Your thumb should be on, or near, the jugular groove, with your fingers on the top ridge of the cervical vertebrae so you cup them with your hand.
3. Slide your hand up the line of vertebrae to the horse's ear, with the heel of the hand applying a slight pressure.
4. Do this a couple of times, and then repeat, but this time opening and closing your thumb and fingers as you slowly travel up the neck, inching your way along, vertebra by vertebra. Experiment with the pressure you use, as it will vary from horse to horse. Repeat four to five times, giving the horse time to process the information before switching sides.

This simple exercise can be done in hand or when the horse is under saddle. Support the rein with the outside hand and run the other hand up the line of the vertebrae, starting from the base of the neck. Panj is releasing his neck and lengthening through the topline. Make sure you do not inadvertently pull the horse towards you, and support the rein across the palm of your hand to ensure that there is not any downward pressure. If the horse pushes into you with his head, hold the leadline or rein nearer the headcollar/bridle, or support his head by resting your fingers lightly on the noseband.

the horse may develop in confidence more quickly when hacking if you can ride out in the company of a steady horse with a sensible rider.

Suggested exercises: Body Wraps, Caterpillar, Ear Work, Promise Wrap, Sliding Numnahs, Stroking the Line, Tail Work, Walking over Plastic, Walking under wands, Walking up Behind, Work over Different Surfaces

STANDING STILL

See also Balance, Feet, picking up, Leading, Mounting, Tying up

Standing still is something we frequently ask our horses to do, on a daily basis and in a wide range of different situations. Although a seemingly simple requirement, in practice it can be very challenging for many horses, and some may struggle to manage it for even a few seconds. Standing still will be difficult for horses which lack muscle and strength, and poor balance is often a major contributory factor. Conformation can also influence the degree of difficulty: horses which have a narrow base of support with their feet placed close together find it much harder to balance.

Other contributory factors include physical issues such as arthritis, back problems, tension through the neck, bitting, dental problems, causing (or anticipation of) discomfort whilst grooming, tacking up or mounting, and poorly fitting saddlery; also an unbalanced rider or handler, and poor aid application. Seek professional assistance from your vet, saddler, equine dental technician and riding instructor to help you in identifying and remedying any of these problems if you suspect they may be creating difficulties for your horse.

influence on how well and easily your horse comes into a halt, and the length of time he can remain in it. Common rider problems include leaning backwards, gripping inwards or upwards with the legs and heels, slouching through the upper body, using over-strong or jerky rein aids, and drawing the hands backwards.

Try to think about your horse moving forwards into the halt, rather than coming back to it; asking for a more gradual transition initially will help. Try also sitting lighter, rather than deeper into the saddle, imagining that you are being gently lifted by a small wave passing underneath it. Staying in balance with the movement is also important as it can be very easy to get left behind; ask someone on the ground to check your position. Another useful tip is to breathe out as you ask for a halt, as this will help you – and your horse – to relax.

By keeping your shoulders, arms, wrists and fingers relaxed, your rein signals will be more subtle and less likely to create resistance. Using a Balance Rein (*see* problem 'Balance, on the Forehand') can be really helpful, as it will encourage the horse to rock on to his hindquarters as he comes into the halt, instead of leaning on your hands (which can cause him to become tight in his jaw and jammed through his neck), or bracing on to, or braking with, his front legs.

Work on improving the horse on the ground in hand, too, as this will help you make more rapid progress with work under saddle.

Suggested exercises: Floating Forwards, Meet and Melt, Neutral Pelvis, Promise Wrap, Reverse Reins, Stroking the Reins, Tail Circles, Tail Glides

Halting while Ridden

Your own posture and aids will have a big

Halting in Hand

The way you lead and handle the horse can

EXERCISE: PROMISE WRAP

Using a body wrap when riding brings new awareness to the horse of his body. It increases balance, co-ordination, and the ability to use his quarters and back, all of which will help increase activity if you have a horse that is inclined to be lazy, as well as improving his halts. In addition it can have a calming effect on nervous or spooky horses, who will also find it hard to stand still. Although most horses accept a wrap quite well, for safety you should always introduce this exercise in easy stages in hand before trying it under saddle. You will need an elasticated 4in (10cm)-wide exercise bandage or an ace wrap (see Chapter 5, section 'Equipment'): because it is stretchy, it will move with your horse, maintaining a constant contact with his body. You will also need an assistant to help you.

1. Attach one end of the bandage to the off-side saddle girth strap using a quick release knot. Keeping hold of the other end, carefully bring it around the quarters over

TOP: *Ask a helper to hold the horse and tie one end of the wrap to the girth straps on the opposite side of the saddle. Bring the wrap round the hindquarters and hold the end. Ask your helper to walk the horse forwards. Halt and repeat the exercise a few times, and ensure that you and the helper are on the same side of the horse.*

MIDDLE: *If the horse is happy with the wrap round his hindquarters, thread the end of the wrap through the girth strap and tie it with a quick-release knot.*

BOTTOM: *You can use the wrap for schooling and when out on a hack to improve balance and give the horse more confidence.*

the top of the tail to the near side. Ask your assistant to walk a few steps forwards and then halt again while you keep a light tension on the bandage so it stays in contact with the horse's quarters.

Your assistant should stay level with the horse's head, and lead from the same side as the one you are on. Walk parallel to the horse's sides rather than his quarters, in case he takes exception to the feel of the wrap and kicks out. If necessary, hold it a little more loosely until he is more confident about this new sensation. If he continues to be concerned, ask your vet to check him over as it can indicate a physical problem that needs attention.

2. Try several transitions between walk and halt. It is often on the second or third time of asking that you get a true reaction; also, if the horse starts to engage very strongly from behind and your saddle tree is a little narrow, it could cause him to buck, so it is important not to skip these introductory stages in hand. If the horse is quite relaxed about this, lift his tail over the top of the bandage and repeat the transitions.

3. If he is still settled, tie the bandage on to the near side of the rear girth strap, again using a quick release knot. The wrap should be snug but not tight around the quarters, and lie about halfway between the point of buttock and the gaskin. As well as halting and walking, introduce a few strides of trot.

4. Provided he's happy about this, you can mount and ride him in the wrap, asking for upward and downward transitions to and from halt. You should feel that he is more engaged, better balanced and has more movement through his back, all of which will contribute to improved and easier transitions.

have a dramatic effect on his balance, and consequently his ability to stop. Adopting the following methods should make a noticeable difference:

- Clip the leadrein to the side ring of the headcollar noseband, rather than to the one beneath the lower jaw
- Stay forwards, by the horse's head. If you are positioned between his eye and shoulder, you will tend to pull at him in either a backwards and/or sideways direction, causing him to become off balance and making it harder for him to stop when you ask
- Hold the leadrein so it passes from the headcollar, between your thumb and index finger, and across your palm; like this, any tension in your wrists will be minimized, enabling you to give more subtle signals
- Keep your feet moving until your horse has completely stopped, as this will help you to stay balanced and your signals to remain smooth. Stopping abruptly will make you stiff, less co-ordinated, and more likely to pull, all of which are likely to be mirrored by your horse
- Carry a wand (see Wand Work, in the problem 'Grooming issues') to help you to slow and halt your horse
- Keep the horse's head and neck straight – if you flex them towards you he is likely to swing his quarters outwards, load the shoulder closest to you, and become progressively more unbalanced

Using a verbal command as well as a physical cue can also be helpful. Keep your voice low-pitched and soothing, draw out the syllables, and use two words rather than one: for example 'aaaand whoaaaa'. The 'aaaand' part of the command gives the horse warning that a command is about to follow, so he has a chance to prepare himself for it. At the same time as you say the word 'aaaand', slacken

EXERCISE: TAIL WORK

Tail work can help relax tight back and neck muscles, and the effect can be felt along the whole spine, right up to the atlas.

1. Stand to the rear and slightly to one side of the quarters. Place one hand lightly on the quarters and gently take small strands of tail hairs between the fingers and thumb of the other hand and gently stroke out along them. Start close to the roots and stroke along the whole length of each strand.

2. Next, take hold of the tail bone with both hands, placing one hand about eight inches (20cm) from the top, and the other about four inches (10cm) lower down. Stand with your feet placed comfortably apart, one foot slightly further forward than the other, with your weight equally distributed between the two. Very slowly apply a gradual, steady but gentle tension to the tail by gradually shifting your weight back over your rear foot.

TOP: *Start by simply stroking the tail hair, strand by strand. Keep to one side and, resting one hand on the pelvis, use your other hand to pick up the hair and slide your fingers from the base of the hair to the tip.*

BOTTOM: *If the horse is happy having his tail handled, support the tail with one hand on the underside of the dock and hold the tail bone in the other hand. Gently move the tail into the shape of a question mark if possible, and circle it in one direction and then the other. You may notice that the tail moves more easily in one direction than the other.*

3. Pause for four or five seconds, then very slowly release the gentle pressure by allowing your weight to move forwards over your front foot. It is essential that you do this exercise very slowly and gently, using the action of your upper body moving over your rear foot and then forward to your front foot rather than pulling with your hands. Do not release the tail abruptly or suddenly. Always keep it aligned with the rest of the spine; do not twist it or draw it to one side.

4. If your horse tries to move forwards or sideways, apply less traction. If the tail feels floppy and slack, try holding it in the same way as in step 2, but gently push it in towards the body rather than taking it outwards away from it. If the tail is very clamped, return to stroking out strands of hair as in step 1, and then try the Tail Rolling exercise instead (*see* problem 'Stiffness').

5. Next try circling the tail by placing a hand under the dock near the top, and the other further down; create a gentle arched shape by lifting up slightly with the top hand and pushing slightly in with the lower hand. If the tail is stiff, don't try and force it to bend. Circle the tail slowly in both directions, keeping the circles small and within a comfortable range of movement.

TOP: *Support the tail between two hands and stand with one foot forward and your other foot back. Transfer your weight from your front foot to your back foot, drawing the tail with you.*

BOTTOM: *Hold for a moment, then slowly shift your weight forwards on to the foot that is forward. You should notice movement through the horse's back and neck as the muscles lift and release.*

the tension on the lead- or bridle rein; then as you say the word 'whoaaaa', close your fingers and give a gentle signal, followed immediately by a slackening of the tension once again. It is vital to remember this release, because this is when your horse will come to a stop, whether you are riding or leading him. If he finds it hard to halt in hand, using the Labyrinth exercise will help improve focus and balance.

Suggested exercises: Forelock Circles and Slides, Labyrinth, Leg Circles, Solo Polework, Sternum Lifts, Stroking the Line, Tail Work, Walking the S, Wither Rocking

STEREOTYPIES
See also Balance, lack of emotional, Bullying, Separation anxiety

A stereotypy is a compulsive, pointless, repetitive action; although most commonly seen in stabled horses, it may persist when the horse is turned out in the field if it has become an established pattern of behaviour. The most commonly seen stereotypies are box walking, crib biting, fence walking, weaving and windsucking.

Box walking: The horse may pace back and forth by the door, or do a complete circuit of the stable. It can lead to fatigue and ligament and joint damage, and if the horse always moves in the same direction, can cause unevenly developed musculature.

Crib biting or cribbing: The horse rests his upper teeth on a stationary object such as the top of the door or his manger, and then, arching his neck, takes a gulp of air, producing a distinctive grunting sound as he does so. The air is not actually swallowed. The muscles on the underside of the neck may become over developed, and damage caused to the incisor teeth.

Fence walking: As with box walking, the horse repetitively walks back and forth along by the gate or an area of fencing, often wearing a distinct track.

Weaving: The horse rocks from side to side, swinging his head and neck from side to side at the same time: sometimes the movement can be very exaggerated. It can cause uneven wear on shoes and damage to limbs and feet.

Windsucking: This habit is similar to cribbing, but the horse doesn't need to use a stationary object to brace against as he gulps the air.

Stereotypies are a response to stress, pain and fear: once they have become an established habit they can be very difficult to resolve even when the initial trigger has been removed, so are best prevented from arising in the first place.

Traditional methods of dealing with stereotypies is usually directed towards stopping the symptom of the behaviour rather than dealing with the underlying cause(s). The use of taste deterrents and devices such as cribbing collars, anti-weaving grids and placing obstacles in the stable usually only have a short-lived success and may even cause the horse to adopt a different stereotypy. Studies indicate that stress hormones are highest just before the action is performed, and lowest just after; so physically preventing the behaviour can cause frustration and a consequent increase in stress, and therefore actually increase the urge to perform the stereotypy.

Preventing such behaviours from starting, as well as taking action if they already exist, will require that you closely examine every aspect of the horse's care including environment, companionship, diet and training, and initiate changes where necessary to eliminate or minimize stressors in his life.

Many stereotypies are due to easily avoidable poor management practices such as over confinement, lack of exercise, hunger, boredom and lack of companionship. The natural state of being for a horse is an almost constant gentle movement as he selectively browses in the company of his friends, and depriving him of any of these elements is likely to lead to behavioural issues. Turn him out for as much of the time as possible, and when it is necessary to stable him, enrich his environment by ensuring he has access to adequate amounts of forage, and by providing toys such as 'horseballs' and feed balls. Turnips, swedes and other roots and leafy vegetables can also be scattered around the floor for him to 'discover'. Do not place his forage all in the same area, but at several places around the stable so he can move from one to the next, mimicking a grazing pattern; choice is also something he is accustomed to when out at grass, and supplying two or three choices of forage when stabled has been shown to help in reducing stereotypies. Another study indicated that horses that had more contact with people were also less likely to engage in stereotypies, so spending time doing a little TTEAM body work with the horse will help reduce stress levels in more ways than one.

Do not isolate him from other equines; horses do not copy others that exhibit stereotypies, and unless intimidation by a neighbour is the cause of the problem,

EXERCISE: TAIL ROLLING

This very simple exercise will help release tight back muscles and free the horse through his hips.

1. Standing to the rear and one side, take hold of the tail at the top of the dock.
2. Slowly move the tail from side to side using a gentle rolling action. As you work, you should see the horse gradually beginning to swing gently through the quarters, and then through the ribcage and the shoulders.

Stand to one side of the horse and put one hand on his hindquarters to keep a connection and let him know that you are there. This will also enable you to feel any movement in the hind leg, which may indicate concern. Hold the top of the tail with the other hand, but do not lift the tail from the tail groove. Gently roll the tail from one side to another to release tension from the dock. Some horses are supple in the tail, but many are tight and jam the tail tighter into the tail groove when the tail is handled. This exercise helps to release a tight back and is an excellent starting point for tail work.

segregating him may make matters worse. Stable mirrors may also help in reducing stereotypical behaviour, although care must be taken to site them away from food areas. Take into consideration the stable's location, too: depending on the individual, some horses may benefit from being in a busy area where there is plenty of activity to watch, while others may prefer a quieter environment.

Suggested exercises: Belly Lifts, Ear Work, Labyrinth, Mouth Work, Stroking the Line, Tail Work

STIFFNESS
See also Crookedness, Laziness, Outline

Horses can be longitudinally as well as laterally stiff, and may also experience joint stiffness. Tellington TTouches (*see* Chapter 5) can be invaluable as a way of relieving discomfort in stiff, sore muscles after a demanding workout, and also as part of a pre-work warm-up to help loosen up the horse. Stiffness will obviously affect the horse's balance, agility, athleticism and willingness, and it is important not to demand too much too soon of a stiff horse, as he will then associate the

EXERCISE: PICK UP STICKS

This exercise is useful for teaching the horse to look after himself and be more surefooted when hacking out over unlevel ground; because the poles are all set at different distances and angles to each other he will have to think very carefully about his foot placement.

Before attempting this particular ground-work exercise, the horse should first be coping confidently and successfully with less complex pole arrangements such as are found in the exercises Solo Polework (*see* problem 'Clumsiness'), Raised Polework ('Canter, favouring one lead') or ZigZag ('Jumping, running out').

1. Arrange the poles randomly, starting with just a few, lying flat on the floor and with fairly large gaps between them. Lead the horse over them from different directions and angles, so it varies every time.
2. Once the horse is coping confidently and successfully with these, gradually increase the complexity by adding more poles. Try raising the ends of a few by a couple of inches, so he also has random heights as well as spaces to think about.

3. Make sure the exercise is done slowly, as the horse will need to move with precision and accuracy. Don't restrict his headcarriage, but allow him to lower his head as this will make it easier for him to choose where to place his feet and to organize his balance better.

When your horse is confident about walking over a line of poles you can teach him to walk over a random pattern of poles, building up the exercise to make it more complex over several sessions if necessary.

discomfort that he experiences with the work asked of him, and this may lead to unwanted behaviours.

It is also important not to confuse generalized stiffness due to bony changes and arthritic and other conditions that cause discomfort and limit movement, with lack of suppleness, incorrect muscle development and inadequate schooling; ask your vet to examine the horse if you are in any doubt.

Suggested exercises: Caterpillar, Jellyfish Jiggles, Leg Circles, Lick of the Cow's Tongue, Tail work, Tail Rolling, Walking the S

STUMBLING
See also Balance, Clumsiness, Outline

Potential causes of stumbling might include poor shoeing, fatigue, an unbalanced rider, and a momentary loss of concentration, as well as physical problems such as lameness and arthritis. It is also often linked with a lack of co-ordination, a poor proprioceptive sense, a poor outline and being on the forehand. The use of half halts, and schooling exercises such as transitions (particularly walk to trot) and lateral work aimed at freeing the shoulders and lightening the forehand may be beneficial.

Polework exercises can also be excellent for developing balance, co-ordination and concentration, and increasing spatial awareness: with young horses they can be an excellent way of educating the body and providing mental stimulus without overstressing immature joints.

Suggested exercises: Balance Rein, Body Wraps, Leg Circles, Pick Up Sticks, Sternum Lifts, Wand Work

TACKING UP, DIFFICULTIES IN
See Bridle, difficult to, and Saddle, difficult to

TEETH, GRINDING
See also Stereotypies

Although grinding the teeth can be a stereotypical behaviour in some horses, it is usually an indication of pain, which may be in the mouth; it has also been linked with gastric discomfort – though it may, of course, be due to pain anywhere in the body. It is often accompanied by a bobbing movement of the head, laid back ears and tail swishing.

Grinding the teeth can also be a sign of tension and stress caused by factors such as the proximity of other horses, the stable environment and management, poor rein management and/or forceful aid application by the rider, and difficulty in coping with the work asked of him.

Suggested exercises: Ear Work, Lick of the Cow's Tongue, Mouth Work, Tail Work

TEETH, HOLDING ON TO BIT WHEN UNBRIDLING
See Bridle, difficult to

TRAFFIC SHY
See also Spookiness, Standing still

With a horse that has severe problems on the road it must be considered whether it is either practical or safe to attempt to help him overcome his concerns. It may be possible to avoid busy roads, but quiet leafy lanes can be just as dangerous, with high hedges and overhanging trees casting shadows across the road, as well as sharp bends and other hazards which limit a driver's ability to see you.

Furthermore, many drivers use smaller roads to avoid more congested areas, and drive without any thought as to what animals might be in the road ahead – and because lanes are often narrow, choices as to getting out of the way quickly may be severely limited. Added to this, the horse may be more spooky on a quiet road due to hidden gateways and livestock grazing in the fields – and even quiet horses have been severely injured or killed due to driver error.

Horses that are fearful of traffic are usually tight in the tail, have restricted movement in the back, lack hind-limb engagement and are unsettled in the yard and/or when working in hand. They may also work in a consistently high-headed frame, and be worried by movement behind them.

If you really want or need to address this problem it is of paramount importance that you work regularly and methodically in a quiet environment to improve the horse's posture, self confidence and self control. You cannot do this simply through riding, but will need to spend time doing body-work and ground-work exercises, and on working on your own levels of confidence too, since any anxiety you may have will exacerbate the horse's fears.

Use all the exercises listed below, and be creative in the way that you help the horse by exposing him to as many novel sights as possible whilst working in the safety of his home. It can be worth contacting your local riding club to see if they offer any road-work sessions, and to employ the help of a professional who uses quiet and positive techniques to help you and your horse.

As well as working on the horse's posture from the ground, accustom him to being ridden in the Promise Wrap (*see* problem 'Standing still – halting while ridden'), and work through the exercise suggested here, so that he learns to remain calm if something approaches him from behind.

If you feel you are making progress, try to broaden his experience by working in the yard or field in the company of traffic that you can control. If you cannot use a car, ask someone to ride a quad bike or a tractor perhaps, and give a clear signal to the driver if you want him to stop. Pay close attention to your horse's body language, and do not attempt to progress too quickly. By all means use feed to encourage him to chew and to breathe, but pick something

EXERCISE: WALKING UP BEHIND

Some horses panic when there is movement behind them, and this exercise is an excellent way to teach a horse to turn his head and look when something is moving behind him, and build up his confidence, rather than spinning round or bolting. It is also useful for horses that are difficult to catch, or those that swing their hindquarters to you when you enter the stable, and is a practical first step if you want to long-line a horse. Moreover if you have the misfortune to fall off your horse on a narrow track and end up behind him, you will be very grateful that you taught him this simple exercise!

You will need a helper, some treats (*see* Clicker Targeting, Chapter 5), and to have practised leading your horse from both sides, using a wand if possible (*see* problem 'Leading issues').

1. Ask your helper to walk the horse forwards. Walk behind him, out to the side where he can see you, and making sure that you are outside kicking range. Talk to him so that he knows you are there. For safety, only approach the horse on the same side as the handler so that if he moves away from you if he is worried he can do so without treading on or running into the handler. If he is really nervous about having someone behind him you may have to start this exercise by walking parallel to his ribs or even in line with his shoulder, gradually moving back over several sessions. Horses that have had problems on the lunge or loading may be nervous about having someone to the side or behind them, so read the horse's body language at all times.

2. If he is rushing, ask him to 'Whoa' after a couple of paces, but if he is not showing

any concern let him walk on for a little longer before asking him to stop. Give a clear voice signal so that he can hear you and respond accordingly, and to let the handler know that you are going to ask the horse to stop. Say 'Aaaand whoooooaaaaa', drawing out the syllables so that the signal is not abrupt. Allow him time to organize his body; if he doesn't understand what you want him to do, the handler can back up your voice signal with the wand and/or a gentle ask-and-release signal on the leadline.

TOP: Ask a helper to walk the horse forwards, and walk up behind him. Ask the horse to 'whoooaaa', and ask the helper to back up the signal with the wand and leadline if necessary. Stay slightly out to the side so that the horse can see you, and do not take him by surprise.

3. As your horse starts to slow or preferably halt, walk up to his head calmly and offer him a piece of food. Don't worry if he swings his body away from you initially, as this is a common response in nervous and/or stiff horses. Repeat this exercise a few times on one side, and if the horse is comfortable being led from both sides, continue this exercise on the other side. He should quickly learn that someone approaching from behind is nothing to fear, but is in fact a rewarding experience, and that a tasty treat will follow if he stops when he hears the words 'Aaaaand whooooa'.

BELOW: As the horse stops, hold out a treat in your hand and encourage him to turn his head to take the treat. Repeat this exercise from both sides, but remember to keep the handler on the same side as you, to prevent an accident occurring if the horse swings his body away.

4. Continue to build on this exercise over several days. The aim is to teach the horse to stop and simply turn his head for the treat, rather than swinging his body away from you. As the horse develops confidence, speed up your own pace so that you can walk quickly up behind him and ultimately run up behind him without alarming him – though avoid the temptation to rush through these steps. The aim is to teach him to stop purely on the voice cue without any intervention from the handler.

that will not cause him to choke if he grabs it too quickly, which can be a sign of concern.

If you are ready to go out on the road, ask a friend with a steady, reliable horse to accompany you, and use a body wrap attached to the saddle to give your horse more confidence. Keep the ride short, and remember that any tension in your own body will transfer to your horse, so sing or talk to him so that you remember to breathe.

Wear high visibility clothing and a tabard that asks drivers to give you plenty of room. Ask traffic to slow down, but remember that large vehicles have air brakes that might cause your horse to spook. Take advantage of driveways and gateways to let traffic pass, and turn your horse so that he can see them. If you have not taught your horse to stand quietly when asked to do so at home, it is unlikely that he will stand still when he is out and about, so if necessary add this to your list of 'things to teach' before you venture out.

Suggested exercises: Balance Rein, Belly Lifts, Body Wraps, Caterpillar, Crest Release, Ear Work, Labyrinth, Mouth Work, Rotating the Pelvis, Sliding Numnahs, Tail Work, Walking over Plastic, Walking Up Behind, Wither Rocking, Work over Difficult Surfaces

TRAVELLING
See also Balance, Bullying, Claustrophobia, Doors, Standing still, Tying up

Travelling can be highly stressful even for an experienced horse – don't make the mistake of thinking that just because he is compliant and loads without fuss the experience isn't a challenging one. Discomfort from excess cold or heat, flooring which is slippery or noisy, toxic gases from exhaust fumes or the build-up of waste products, isolation from his companions, external noise and unpredictable movement can all contribute to making the experience unpleasant. Signs that your horse has had a

stressful trip include scrabbling around, kicking, sweating up, shaking, and exhibiting hesitancy about loading again. If you suspect he's had a bad journey, don't ignore the warning signs: go back to basics, practising loading and unloading and creating pleasant associations – plus, of course, investigating the possible causes for his reluctance.

With a horse that is inclined to be difficult, it's worth spending some time and effort working on improving matters, rather than waiting until the problem has escalated to the point where he is impossible to load without resorting to coercion. An important part of any loading re-training programme is to try to work out just why the horse is so reluctant to co-operate. 'Difficult' horses usually have a perfectly legitimate reason for their behaviour, even if it isn't always immediately apparent to you, so be prepared to be open-minded and patient, and remember that sometimes there may be not just one, but several contributory factors.

The following 'top ten' causes of loading difficulties will give you a starting point from which to try to work out why there is a problem, if one exists – and will help you to keep trouble-free horses exactly that way: without a problem.

1. **Poor driving skills:** If a horse has had a bad ride, it's not surprising if subsequently he doesn't want to go back into the vehicle again to repeat the experience. It only takes one bad journey to shake a horse's confidence – or to shatter it completely if he's already a bit anxious. Clipping kerbs, bumpy showgrounds, abrupt braking and acceleration, and taking turns too fast – none of which he will be able to anticipate – will give the horse a less than comfortable or confidence-inspiring ride.

2. **Unpleasant associations** with a trailer or lorry may make the horse reluctant to load, and may not always be related to

what happens during the actual journey or loading process. One extremely competitive owner would travel her horse on most weekends – sometimes on both days – to shows or to clinics. Although she enjoyed these outings, her horse was less enthusiastic, and it didn't take long for him to realize that every time he went into the vehicle it was to go off for another hard work session, with the result that he became progressively more and more difficult to load for the outward journey, although no problem at all when coming home.

3. **Bullying:** Travelling companions need to be chosen with care; the presence of a confident horse may give a nervous one reassurance, but it can backfire if the behaviour of the poor traveller ends up frightening the good one. As an alternative, fitting a stable mirror to the interior of the vehicle has been successful in helping some horses to relax during a journey.

   Friction can also arise between individuals when placed in such a confined space and in such close proximity to each other. An owner who took a friend's horse along with hers to a competition was horrified to find on arrival that it had attacked hers over the top of the partition, leaving one side of his neck cut and bleeding to the extent of requiring veterinary attention; for some time after this experience he was extremely reluctant to enter the vehicle again. Obviously this is an extreme example, but bullying, even on a less dramatic level, can occur without the driver necessarily being aware of it at the time; even where high partitions prevent actual physical contact and injury, they won't necessarily prevent some degree of intimidation from occurring.

4. **Space:** Ensuring that your horse has ample room is essential, both in terms of length and of headroom, and also enough space widthways so that he can spread his legs in order to help balance himself. Partitions often don't make enough allowance for this, and if a gap is present at the bottom, the horse's feet can slide beneath them and become wedged, causing a major panic. As well as partitions to the sides, containment to the rear needs to be considered: use a body wrap to prepare the horse for the feel of the breeching strap in a trailer. A webbing tailgate is often better as it is softer and will have a slight amount of 'give' as compared to the usual plastic or rubber-covered chain arrangement.

5. **Travelling clothes:** Travelling boots can offer good leg protection, and are quick and easy to clean and to put on and take off, but they need to be comfortable and a really good fit. They also need to be very secure, with no risk of them slipping down, as this may cause the horse to become restless or even to panic. Bandages may be more suitable in some cases, as they conform better to the leg; it is advisable to secure fastening tapes with electrical tape over the top. Whatever clothing is worn, the horse should first be accustomed to wearing it in less stressful circumstances.

   Don't load or travel your horse wearing his saddle, as this will reduce the amount of space he has to each side.

6. **Careless loading:** Many horses fear getting their hip bones banged, particularly if this has happened in other situations, such as going through stable doors or gateways. With trailers in particular, room for manoeuvring the horse in and out, whether by way of a front- or rear-unload ramp, can sometimes be tight, even when partitions have been moved across. Care needs to be taken to guide the horse as straight and slowly as possible, to prevent

him from accidentally stepping off the side of the ramp as well as to avoid bumping his sides or quarters.

7. **The ramp** can be another source of much anxiety, especially if it 'bounces' slightly beneath the horse's weight, giving him the impression that this particular piece of ground is not very safe to stand on. This feeling of insecurity can also persist once inside, and if the horse starts to fidget will further increase the amount of movement which occurs. Lorry ramps are heavier than those on trailers and give a more solid feeling beneath the feet, as does the floor of the vehicle – although sometimes the ramp can be quite steep.

   Some horses find the change in sound as their hooves leave solid ground and move on to the ramp alarming: make sure the ramp also offers good grip for the feet. Drawing some bedding down from inside the lorry or trailer can help muffle the sound and provide better footing. If your horse has concerns about the ramp, it may be helpful to teach the exercise Work over Difficult Surfaces (*see* problem 'Bolting, while ridden'). Include a solid piece of non-slip wood as one of your surfaces: once the horse steps on to a flat board without concern you can progress to a strong, solid, raised wooden platform that will not creak or crack under his weight, and is wide enough for him to be able to step up and on to it with at least two front feet. As well as being an excellent intermediary stage for horses that have loading issues, it is also useful for teaching them how to cross a wooden bridge calmly when out hacking.

8. **The vehicle:** Some horses may be happier in a trailer, others in a lorry – each has points for and against, and you may need to try both in order to discover which the horse prefers. A trailer ramp is less steep than a lorry's but may give less feeling of solidity underfoot; and a trailer can be more exposed to exterior noise, and you have no choice in how the horse is positioned inside it.

   Studies have shown that horses facing forwards tend to move more due to difficulty in balancing, while those travelled facing to the rear found it easier to balance and had a lower heart rate. Although a few makes of trailer are available designed specifically to permit rear-facing travel, in the majority the horses face forwards. The hardest way for a horse to travel is in a horizontal position – that is, standing across the lorry in a straight line – and a herringbone design is far better. With trailers, problems can arise if the hitch is adjusted too high or too low, if the towing vehicle is underpowered, or from snaking.

   A lorry tends to give a smoother ride, and a fidgety horse or a sidewind is less likely to disturb the balance of the vehicle; but the interior may be darker and less inviting, the ramp is steeper, and ventilation is sometimes poor.

   When practising loading with a trailer, ensure minimum movement by putting down corner jacks for stability as well as the jockey wheel; make sure it is chocked up, too, so there is no backward or forward movement.

   Make the interior as inviting as possible, positioning the vehicle so that as much light as possible is allowed in; do not leave the groom's door open, however, as horses have been known to try to escape through it. A light-coloured bedding will also help; wood chips are a good choice as they won't tangle round the feet as straw can.

9. **Poor balance:** A common cause of a poor traveller is because the horse has difficulty balancing whilst the vehicle is on the move. One hour's journey is considered

to be the equivalent of an hour of walking exercise, but it could potentially be even more demanding, as the more the horse struggles to maintain his balance, the greater the physical and mental demands placed on him. Teaching him how to adjust his balance through the use of exercises such as Sternum Lifts (*see* problem 'Balance, lack of physical'), Wither Rocking (problem 'Feet, difficult to pick up') and Shoulder Presses ('Jogging') will help him to make subtle postural adjustments which will make journeys less frightening as well as physically less demanding.

The horse will also need to be able to move his head and neck to help him balance. Although you will need to tie him up short enough to prevent him turning round or getting his head caught under the rope, it mustn't interfere with his balance, or pull him forwards against the breastbar.

10. **Physical problems** are also often overlooked as a possible cause of difficulties. One mare that was difficult both to load and unload was not being obstinate as her owners had supposed, but was in fact suffering from a back problem – once it had been diagnosed and resolved they had no further difficulties. Ear infections may also cause difficulties in balancing whilst the vehicle is on the move.

Achieving Success

Brute force is never the answer to solving the problem, and resorting to coercion will only create and reinforce bad associations. It can also be dangerous and result in injury to the horse and/or handler; while other non-force methods such as deprivation of water are inhumane as well as potentially harmful to health.

If you encounter difficulties, don't dismiss it as stubbornness, but investigate all possible causes, try to make your vehicle as pleasant an environment as possible, and break down re-training into easy stages. There are no quick fixes: many people do not connect riding and handling problems with travelling ones, but these are areas you may need to address in order to achieve success.

Working through all the exercises suggested will be good preparation for loading, helping the horse to develop greater confidence, and in building trust between you both. When you return to practising loading again with a vehicle, take your time, and don't worry if at first the horse doesn't go in completely.

Suggested exercises: Body Wrap, Clicker Targeting, Narrow Spaces Exercise, Solo Polework, Stroking the Line, Walking over Plastic, Walking Under Wands, Work over Different Surfaces

TRIMMING UP
See also Clipping

Before you decide to pull your horse's mane or tail, do ask yourself whether it's really necessary to remove his natural protection from insects and the weather: a plaited tail can look just as smart as a pulled one at shows. A very long or heavy mane can interfere with rein management, or make the horse hot in warm weather, but putting it into a few loosely plaited pigtails at the withers, or a running crest plait, can solve the problem. If you feel it is necessary to thin and shorten the mane, rather than pulling it – which many horses find painful, even if it is done when the horse is warm after exercise – a better tolerated option for many, and one which works well, is to use a mane-thinning comb. If the horse shakes his head when you touch his mane, start by stroking small strands of the hairs and then progress to circling them and gently sliding your fingers from the base to the tip of the mane, taking the hair in an upward direction.

EXERCISE: WALKING UNDER WANDS

This exercise has so many practical applications that we feel every horse should learn to do it! It is a valuable step when starting or restarting horses under saddle, helps horses overcome concerns about walking under hanging boughs or under door lintels, gives horses that spook more confidence, and can be incorporated into other ground-work exercises for horses that are reluctant loaders. It helps nervous horses develop more confidence, and is a useful exercise for horses that find it hard to stand at the mounting block.

Depending on the horse, you will need at least two helpers, plus two mounting blocks or some other stable, raised platform, and two wands (long dressage schooling sticks). As well as teaching horses to walk under the wands, you can also teach them to walk under coloured pool noodles using the same steps and principles.

If the horse is particularly nervous and/or difficult to lead, first teach him to work between two handlers as described in the Homing Pigeon exercise (*see* problem 'Leading issues'); you will also need to teach him the exercise Wand Work (*see* problem 'Grooming issues') before you attempt to teach him this exercise.

1. Place two blocks parallel to each other, and wide enough apart to give the horse and handler(s) plenty of room when walking between them. Lead the horse around the blocks first, and then walk between them, asking him to halt before, between and after passing through. If he cannot halt he is nervous, and will need to be led around them and through them while they are more widely spaced apart before you can progress.

2. Once the horse can walk and halt calmly between the blocks, and from both directions, ask one helper to stand next to one of the blocks holding a wand

ABOVE: *Once the horse is able to walk between the two blocks, ask another helper to stand next to one block with the wand held in front of them.*

LEFT: *Build up the exercise by adding another person on the other side, and progress to having your helpers stand on the blocks. If the horse remains calm, ask the helpers to hold the wands higher and at a slight angle towards each other.*

vertically in front of them with the button end resting on the floor. Repeat the earlier steps, halting before, between and after the blocks, and if your horse is relaxed about this, ask the second helper to stand next to the other block, directly opposite the first helper, and holding their wand in the same position.

Both the helpers should have some food in their pockets so they can give a small treat to the horse if he is worried. This will help him to grow in confidence and also encourages him to turn his head in both directions to look at the wands and the people. If he gets really pushy, don't use the food, or offer a low value treat such as hay.

3. If this does not cause the horse any concern, ask one helper to stand on the block and repeat the exercise. When the horse is happy about this, the second handler can do the same; they should still be holding the wands vertically in front of them.

Remember to walk the horse past the blocks and helpers from both directions and ask him to halt at different stages. He should be able to stand quietly between two handlers standing on the blocks before you progress further, and it may take several short sessions to achieve this. When your horse has reached this stage, ask one handler to hold the wand pointing vertically up in the air. Repeat the steps as before, and ask the second handler to do the same if your horse is confident. If at any stage the horse panics, go back a step.

4. Once the horse can walk past the two raised wands, ask the handlers to hold their wands high in the air with the tips pointing towards each other so that your horse is now walking under them. If he cannot do this, try with one wand. Ask him to halt beneath the wands and remember to ask him to halt again once he has passed them so that you can gauge his level of confidence.

5. The final step is to ask the helpers to hold the wands so that the tips are actually touching. You can develop this further by gradually lowering them slightly to that he learns to lower his head and pass under them without panicking. Once he can walk under the wands, if you want to teach him to walk under coloured pool noodles or something similar, go back to the beginning of the exercise and repeat all the steps with the new equipment.

Progress to having the wands touch each other so that the horse is walking underneath an arch. Offer the horse a treat so that he learns to wait, and actually turn towards each person. If he cannot halt or cannot eat he is concerned, and you will need to go back a few steps to build up his confidence.

Whiskers are sensory 'feeler' hairs which, together with the lips, help the horse to browse safely when grazing, and are best left on: trimming them is a purely cosmetic and entirely unnecessary exercise. Although removal doesn't seem to bother some horses, with others it appears to affect their spatial awareness and even their balance. Cutting off the whiskers is now illegal in Germany.

Suggested exercises: Crest Release, Forelock Circles and Slides, Neck Rocking

TYING UP, HANGING BACK
See also Balance, Separation anxiety, Spookiness, Standing still

Many horses struggle when they are tied up because they find it difficult to stand still due to poor balance, anxiety and/or discomfort. Physical issues in the neck can be another, often overlooked, cause; horses which pull back when tied often have unlevel ears, which can be an indicator of tension, and/or previous damage around the first two cervical vertebrae. A permanently hanging lower lip can also indicate a problem around the poll. Such horses panic when they feel pressure on the headpiece of the headcollar, and may also suddenly 'spook' at the wall, even though they may have been standing there reasonably quietly for some time.

Teaching a horse to stand by tying him 'hard and fast' is asking for trouble because it is more likely to trigger a defensive and instinctive reaction of panic, and could cause serious injury to the horse should he slip, flip over, or damage the sensitive soft tissue in the upper part of the neck.

To help your horse stand quietly when tied you will have to think and work 'outside the box'. The horse uses his neck for balance, and if this is restricted through being tied up he may find it hard to stand quietly. If he is worried by movement behind him he will also

struggle when tied as he may not be able to look around when he is concerned. Horses that are permanently in the flight reflex will struggle with this type of containment; also nervous horses that rely on the company of friends for emotional support may fidget when tied because they may lose sight of their companions.

Exercises aimed at teaching the horse to stand, to work between poles and through narrow spaces, and generally to improve his physical balance and confidence will be a practical starting point when working with a horse that cannot be tied. Wand Work (*see* problem 'Grooming issues') can also be very beneficial, because stroking it down the front of the horse's chest and front legs as well as all over his body can help promote calm and relaxation when you do progress to tying him up. A full or half body wrap (*see* Chapter 5) will not only help to improve his balance, but may help him to settle as well. Clicker training him to stand next to a target in the stable (*see* Chapter 5) is an alternative to teaching the horse to tie up – or if you do want to work through this problem, will provide a very practical way of giving him a different and positive association which can help him overcome his fears.

The Dingo leading exercise (*see* problem 'Leading, Hanging Back') can also be used to teach him to step forwards when he starts to hang back, but it is imperative that this has first been taught in hand. It can help break down the steps to tying even further if you start with a long length of thin, light rope simply threaded through the ring and held by you, as you can give him more slack if he starts to move back, before asking him to step forwards again.

From a safety point of view no horse should be left tied up unattended as a bird, blowing bag, buzzing insect or sting can result in an accident, and of course lead chains, reins or leadropes should never be attached to the bit.

Tie-up rings should be at an appropriate height for the horse, and he should be attached to something that will break in an emergency. If using baler twine, separate out a few strands, as modern nylon twine does not break as easily as old-fashioned string. Clip the leadrope to the side of the headcollar if possible, as this will allow the horse more freedom to look around as well as reducing the amount of pressure on the headpiece of the headcollar if he does move backwards.

Suggested exercises: Dingo, Homing Pigeon, Labyrinth, Leg Circles, Mouth Work, Narrow Spaces Exercise, Tail Work, Walking under Wands, Work over Different Surfaces

WATER, FEAR OF
See also Balance, Clumsiness, Rushing, Spooking

Horses may be fearful of water for a number of reasons, including concern about the movement of the water, or the changing play of light on its surface; there may be negative associations if water has been thrown at them as punishment for kicking at a stable door, for example, or if they've been sprayed in the face with a hosepipe when being washed, or if they've previously had an accident or bad experience when jumping a stream or water jump.

Whatever the reason, it is worth spending time teaching the horse that walking through water is nothing to fear, so that puddles do not become impassable barriers whether on the yard, in a field gateway or out hacking. If this is a serious problem, it is worth investing in a portable water tray. There are plenty available on the market, and if you are on a yard with others you might join together in sharing the investment, as it can be used for ground-work exercises, and at a later date for jumping, too. Purchase a soft-edged tray and not a rigid water jump so that your horse can walk over it safely without giving himself a fright by cracking it.

As with any exercise, when helping a horse to overcome a fear, it is far safer to teach it first from the ground before trying it while mounted. Start by using the water tray empty, setting it up in the same way as the Difficult Surfaces exercise (*see* problem 'Bolting, while ridden') and/or the Walking over Plastic exercise below.

Once your horse is happy walking over the tray, put a small amount of water in it so that he sees some water but its movement is minimal. Gradually build up his confidence over several sessions, increasing the amount of water in the tray each time. Once he is happy to walk through the water, ask him to stand in it for a moment before walking him out. Vary the location of the water tray so that he learns to walk through water in different places.

Suggested exercises: Dingo, Homing Pigeon, Pick Up Sticks, Solo Polework, Stroking the Line, Walking Over Plastic, Wand Work

WEAVING
See Stereotypies

WHIP, FEAR OF
See also Grooming issues

Some horses are whip shy as a result of being punished in the past, but many horses that are fearful of the whip have poor body awareness and may never have been hit at all. Horses that spook often panic if they are touched with a schooling whip, and spending time helping the horse to address this fear will also help with other associated issues, including standing still and a dislike of being groomed.

It is also practical to help a horse that may be whip shy, because for example being touched by a branch when out hacking might panic him. You may also want to be able to use a stick to gently motivate him to walk forwards in hand or under saddle, and it is a really useful tool to have when working the horse through

EXERCISE: WALKING OVER PLASTIC

You will need a helper to move the plastic for you; make sure they do this slowly and that the horse is able to watch them from a safe distance. If no one is available to assist, be prepared to put the horse back in a stable while you work through each of the stages.

1. Lay two sheets of plastic on the ground in an open-ended arrowhead, as shown in the photograph. Weight the plastic with poles to ensure it doesn't move in the wind, as this will spook the horse. Ideally this exercise is best done in an indoor arena or on a calm day.
2. Horses are more visually aware of change than most humans, and the sight of a new object may cause concern, so spend some time walking around the outside of the arrowhead so the horse can study the plastic before you ask him to approach it. If he is noise sensitive the sound of the arena surface flicking up from his hooves and landing on the plastic may make him anxious, so bear this in mind.
3. If the horse will walk quietly past the plastic, next halt in front of it at the widest point of the arrowhead, before asking him to walk slowly through the gap in the centre. Repeat this step, this time asking him to halt on the other side of the arrowhead as well. If he cannot halt it means that he has a level of concern about the plastic, so allow him to walk on and either try again, or go back to walking around the outside.
4. If he is unconcerned, take him through again and ask him to halt midway between the sheets. Make sure that he can stand still, as you want to avoid him swinging his quarters around and stepping on the plastic before he is ready to progress to this part of the exercise. Stroke his legs with the wand and let him look at the plastic. Continue on through the arrowhead, and ask him to stop on the other side. Pay attention to his body language and any quickening in pace, because you want to build his confidence and not overload him, and this may take a few sessions.

Start by leading your horse past plastic sheeting or a plastic water jump on the ground. Allow him to look at the object.

5. If your horse is walking calmly between the two pieces of plastic and can halt and wait for a forward cue before, between and after them, lead him through again, this time walking over a sheet yourself to accustom him to the noise.

6. Narrow the arrowhead a little and lead him through again, repeating the earlier steps. Gradually continue bringing the ends of the plastic closer and closer together, repeating the exercise each time, until finally the sheets are touching. If your horse is still calm you can then ask him to walk across the plastic widthways. You can vary the exercise by asking him to step on to the plastic and then teach him to back off the sheet as well.

Walk the horse over the plastic widthways, and ask him to halt, first on the plastic, and afterwards as well. If the horse cannot halt he is nervous. Avoid letting him paw at the plastic as this may frighten him.

some of the ground-work exercises suggested in this book.

Breaking down the association with a whip needs to be done with great care, patience and understanding. This approach was used successfully on a horse that had been beaten into a slaughter truck and as a result was extremely suspicious of the whip, but this method can also be used with horses that have poor body awareness and may not be able to tolerate the exercise suggested in the section on grooming issues. Safety is essential, so pay attention to the horse's body language at all times, and do not be tempted to rush through the stages.

Start by stroking the horse down his neck with the back of your hand and along the underside of his neck and down his chest. Repeat this a few times, and if he is comfortable with this, lay a piece of straw or even a plastic drinking straw across the palm of your hand, holding it in place with your thumb and repeat the stroking with the back of your hand. Continue to build his confidence, over several days if necessary.

From time to time turn your hand over so that you stroke him with the straw. Gradually increase the length of the straw and progress to a thin, short stick from a tree. Find a broken riding crop and cut it to a reasonable length and continue alternating between stroking him with the back of the hand and then the actual crop. Gradually extend the areas on his body that you touch. Progress to stroking him with a short crop, and finally with a dressage schooling whip.

You can also employ the help of a friend and ask them to use a clicker and some treats to reward the horse while working through these stages, so that he gains a pleasant association with the whip.

Suggested exercises: Body Wraps, Clicker Target Training, Ear Work

WINDSUCKING
See Stereotypies

WOOD CHEWING
See Chewing, Pica

Further Information

FURTHER READING

Bush, Karen and Jenkinson, Steve *The Horse Rider's Hacking Handbook* (Crowood)
Practical advice on riding out with your horse, including dealing with hazards and difficult behaviours.

Bush, Karen and Marczak, Julian *101 Rider Exercises* (David & Charles)
Mounted and dismounted exercises to help develop and improve your position in the saddle.

Cummings, Peggy and Deterding, Deidre *Connected Riding* (Primedia Enthusiast Publications)
Available from www.connectedriding.com

Fisher, Sarah *Know Your Horse Inside Out* (David & Charles)
In-depth information about tension patterns, analysis of body posture and influences on behaviour.

Hood, Robyn *All Wrapped Up for Horses* (Available from the TTEAM UK, Canada or USA offices) More information on Body Wraps.

Kurland, Alexandra *Clicker Training for your Horse* (Ringpress)

Morrison, Liz *Simple Steps to Riding Success* (David & Charles)
Using neuro-linguistic programming to help overcome rider anxieties.

Tellington Jones, Linda with Taylor, Sybil *Getting in Touch with Horses* (Kenilworth Press)
Further information on TTEAM exercises to try with your horse.

Tellington Jones, Linda *Improve Your Horse's Wellbeing* (Trafalgar Square Books)
Further information on TTEAM exercises to try with your horse.

USEFUL CONTACTS AND ADDRESSES

TTEAM UK
Tilley Farm, Farmborough,
Bath, England BA2 0AB
www.tteam.co.uk

TTEAM Canada
5435 Rochdell Road
Vernon, Canada, BC V1B 3E8
www.ttouch.ca

TTEAM USA
PO Box 3793, Santa Fe
USA, NM 87501
www.ttouch.com

Alexander Technique
www.stat.org.uk

Association of Chartered Physiotherapists in
Animal Therapy (ACPAT)
www.acpat.org

Association of Pet Behaviour Counsellors
www.apbc.org.uk

Bach Flower Essences
www.bachcentre.com

Blind/impaired Vision Horses
www.blindhorses.org

British Association of Equine Dental Technicians
www.baedt.com

British Association of Homoeopathic Veterinary
Surgeons
www.bahvs.com

Clicker training
www.theclickercenter.com

Peggy Cummings, Connected Riding
www.connectedriding.com

Farriers Registration Council
www.farrier-reg.gov.uk

Horse & Rider magazine
www.horseandrideruk.com

McTimoney Chiropractic Association
www.mctimoneychiropractic.org
www.mctimoney-animal.org.uk

Probalance Probiotic Equine
www.probalanceuk.com

Royal College of Veterinary Surgeons
www.rcvs.org.uk

Seasonal Affective Disorder (SAD)
Light therapy boxes for hire or purchase
www.sad-lighthire.co.uk

The Stable Mirror Company
www.stable-mirrors.co.uk

Towing Horse Trailers
www.towinghorsetrailers.co.uk

Index